# Developmental Approaches to Giftedness and Creativity

David Henry Feldman, *Editor*

---

**NEW DIRECTIONS FOR CHILD DEVELOPMENT**
WILLIAM DAMON, *Editor-in-Chief*

Number 17, September 1982

Paperback sourcebooks in
The Jossey-Bass Social and Behavioral Sciences Series

Jossey-Bass Inc., Publishers
San Francisco • Washington • London

*Developmental Approaches to Giftedness and Creativity*
Number 17, September 1982
   David Henry Feldman, *Editor*

**New Directions for Child Development Series**
William Damon, *Editor-in-Chief*

**New Directions for Child Development** (publication number
USPS 494-090) is published quarterly by Jossey-Bass Inc., Publishers.
Second-class postage rates are paid at San Francisco, California,
and at additional mailing offices.

*Correspondence:*
Subscriptions, single-issue orders, change of address notices,
undelivered copies, and other correspondence should be sent to
*New Directions* Subscriptions, Jossey-Bass Inc., Publishers,
433 California Street, San Francisco, California 94104.

Editorial correspondence should be sent to the Editor-in-Chief,
William Damon, Department of Psychology, Clark University,
Worcester, Massachusetts 01610.

Library of Congress Catalogue Card Number LC 82-82706

International Standard Serial Number ISSN 0195-2269

International Standard Book Number ISBN 87589-877-7

Cover art by Willi Baum

Manufactured in the United States of America

# Ordering Information

The paperback sourcebooks listed below are published quarterly and can be ordered either by subscription or single-copy.

Subscriptions cost $35.00 per year for institutions, agencies, and libraries. Individuals can subscribe at the special rate of $21.00 per year *if payment is by personal check.* (Note that the full rate of $35.00 applies if payment is by institutional check, even if the subscription is designated for an individual.) Standing orders are accepted.

Single copies are available at $7.95 when payment accompanies order, and *all single-copy orders under $25.00 must include payment.* (California, Washington, D.C., New Jersey, and New York residents please include appropriate sales tax.) For billed orders, cost per copy is $7.95 plus postage and handling. (Prices subject to change without notice.)

To ensure correct and prompt delivery, all orders must give either the *name of an individual* or an *official purchase order number.* Please submit your order as follows:

*Subscriptions:* specify series and subscription year.
*Single Copies:* specify sourcebook code and issue number (such as, CD8).

Mail orders for United States and Possessions, Latin America, Canada, Japan, Australia, and New Zealand to:
Jossey-Bass Inc., Publishers
433 California Street
San Francisco, California 94104

Mail orders for all other parts of the world to:
Jossey-Bass Limited
28 Banner Street
London EC1Y 8QE

## New Directions for Child Development Series
William Damon, *Editor-in-Chief*

CD1  *Social Cognition,* William Damon
CD2  *Moral Development,* William Damon
CD3  *Early Symbolization,* Howard Gardner, Dennie Wolf
CD4  *Social Interaction and Communication During Infancy,* Ina C. Uzgiris
CD5  *Intellectual Development Beyond Childhood,* Deanna Kuhn
CD6  *Fact, Fiction, and Fantasy in Childhood,* Ellen Winner, Howard Gardner
CD7  *Clinical-Developmental Psychology,* Robert L. Selman, Regina Yando
CD8  *Anthropological Perspectives on Child Development,* Charles M. Super, Sara Harkness
CD9  *Children's Play,* Kenneth H. Rubin
CD10 *Children's Memory,* Marion Perlmutter
CD11 *Developmental Perspectives on Child Maltreatment,* Ross Rizley, Dante Cicchetti
CD12 *Cognitive Development,* Kurt W. Fisher

# Contents

The author examines the reasons for studying extraordinariness and finds a relationship between these reasons and research methods A reexamination of the issues leads to a changed conception of giftedness as early promise connected to later creative work and a recommendation for a research strategy that starts with unequivocally extraordinary individuals and works backward.

Based on Piaget's notions of stage, interaction, and transition, an attempt is made to draw implications for studying giftedness and creativity in children. By analyzing the components that enter into the developmental equation, it is possible to diagnose and support early giftedness without resorting to general psychometric predictions. One promising area of investigation is the study of development in nonuniversal domains, the realms within which creative work is actually done.

Using such fields as genetics, neurobiology, and brain science as a basis for discussion, the author proposes a reorganization of competent functioning into seven distinct spheres, each with its own strength, developmental trajectory, and probable areas of application through different symbol systems. By examining extreme cases in each of the proposed realms of competence, it is possible to examine giftedness in a new, more differentiated way.

The author attempts to interpret the common breakdown in performance of musical prodigies as they move from adolescence to adulthood as a confrontation between intuitive, figural competence and newly emerging formal representations. Mature musical performance requires the integration of both kinds of competence, an achievement sometimes beyond the grasp of even the most promising children. To comprehend better the confrontation between systems requires the joint efforts of cognitive developmentalists and those who study the domain of music.

# Foreword

This volume offers some challenging views of giftedness from a group of scholars, most of whom are currently members of the Committee on Development, Giftedness, and the Learning Process of the Social Science Research Council in New York. This committee, appointed by the council in 1980, is exploring new avenues of research to understand the nature and maturation of exceptional abilities and talents. To some extent these chapters bear the fruit of its early deliberations, and while they are rich soil from which new empirical investigations of giftedness may emerge, they also will guide the committee in planning a series of conferences, workshops, and proposals. With the generous support of a grant from the Andrew W. Mellon Foundation, the committee has embarked upon a four-year program of activities to explore many of the themes elaborated in these chapters.

Established in 1924 as a nonprofit, professional organization, the Social Science Research Council is devoted to the interdisciplinary advancement of research in the social sciences. Over its fifty-five year history the council has sought to stimulate new research at the frontiers of thought about man and society — not through the direct support of specific research projects but through the convening of interdisciplinary scholarly groups who examine obstacles to current understanding, chart new research directions, and offer intellectual inspiration to investigators struggling at the fringes of knowledge about human behavior. Through seminars, workshops, training institutes, conferences, and publications, the council has encouraged and facilitated a wide range of theoretical, methodological, and empirical developments in the social sciences. The current objectives of the Committee on Development, Giftedness, and the Learning Process represent a convergence of the Council's long concern with the need to comprehend the processes of human development and its more infrequent efforts to further an understanding of extraordinary talents and abilities, and of the careers of gifted individuals. It is worth noting some of the council's previous efforts in these areas since they also reflect the varied ways in which social scientists have struggled to understand the nature and ontogeny of human abilities.

One of the council's earliest efforts concerned with human development focused on the social and cultural factors that influence personality. The Committee on Culture and Personality included such scholars as Ralph Linton, Robert Redfield, W. I. Thomas, and Edward Sapir, among others, and worked from 1930 to 1940 to help shift the attention of social scientists from speculation about "racial" types of personality to a more scientific search for the socio-

This volume is dedicated to the memory of Halbert B. Robinson.

1

cultural bases of personality. In the 1950s, the council assisted in supporting a team of researchers under the leadership of John Whiting in producing a series of cross-cultural studies on the effects of childrearing practices on personality development. Again, in the 1960s, a council committee under the leadership of sociologist John Clausen attempted to assess and integrate the burgeoning, largely social-psychological, research literature on childhood socialization and published the volume *Socialization and Society* (Clausen, 1968). Children's social and emotional development remains an important research frontier and, in 1976, the council established the Committee on Social and Affective Development During Childhood, which continues to sponsor a wide range of meetings and publications focused on children's emotional and social growth. Other council committees, while not concerned directly with development, have examined research relevant to other aspects of human abilities, including biological considerations (Committee on the Biological Bases of Social Behavior, 1966–1979) and intellective processes (Committee on Intellective Processes, 1959–1964; Committee on Cognitive Research, established in 1972).

In recent years, several council activities have reflected a belief held by an increasing number of social scientists that the study of human behavior and development needs to encompass the entire life span. This concern was represented in the efforts of the Committee of Work and Personality in the Middle Years (1972–1979), which has been succeeded by the Committee on Life Course Perspectives on Middle and Old Age (established in 1977). The latter committee has recently established a subcommittee on child development in a life span perspective that will seek to link child development research with the study of changes in later life.

These council activities reveal the great diversity of viewpoints and knowledge required to understand human development. Many social scientists now contend that to adequately understand a phenomenon requires insights from numerous disciplines, that to ignore one set of variables seriously jeopardizes the validity of scientific findings. For researchers interested in development, this has meant that affect, cognition, social behavior, and cultural contexts cannot be studied in isolation. These domains exist in interaction and must be studied as such. Furthermore, development is most wisely construed as a life-long process, with themes and processes at one period echoing into future patterns while simultaneously reflecting past experiences. It is just such an integrative view of development that the scholars in this volume wish to bring to the study of giftedness. Few researchers have managed to capture the amazing convergence of biological, social, cultural, and psychological factors that characterize the expression of exceptional talent. Even less common are longitudinal investigations that track the course of these talents from their first flowering in childhood to mature expression in a productive and creative career.

Yet it is more than a desire to capture the full complexity of giftedness that inspires these chapters. There is an even more glaring gap in most previous studies of giftedness, a conceptual or definitional flaw that also pervaded the heady and groundbreaking work of the council's Committee on the Early

Identification of Talent (established in the 1950s). Although this group of scholars (which included David McClelland, Frederick Strodtbeck, Leonard Cottrell, Alfred Baldwin, Urie Bronfenbrenner, and Dael Wolfle) grappled productively with a variety of nonintellectual factors in the identification of talent (McClelland and others, 1958), with the notable exception of Urie Bronfenbrenner's innovative studies of individual differences in social sensitivity, they tended to define talent in terms of general academic and occupational achievement. Research on giftedness has been haunted by this notion that children or adults are gifted when they exhibit exceptional performance on measures of general abilities, particularly intellectual ones. This approach has led many developmental researchers to select for study samples of gifted children based upon scores on standardized tests, an approach adopted by Terman in his famous studies and more recently at the University of Washington in a longitudinal study of gifted children initiated by the late Halbert Robinson (Roedell, Jackson, and Robinson, 1980). While this approach has generated considerable wisdom regarding human intellectual development, it has contributed surprisingly little to an understanding of the origins and maturation of exceptional talents and abilities as they are displayed in specific arenas of human endeavor (Terman, 1954).

In actuality, even the layman's use of *gifted* conveys more than intellectual acuity. It signifies a combination of creativity and mastery of skills that is highly domain specific. While there has to some extent been a proliferation and public acceptance of educational programs for the academically gifted child, few educators or parents believe that these students simultaneously possess extraordinary ability in art, music, writing, or athletics. Most research that has addressed this issue suggests only a minimal correlation of general intellectual ability with gifted performance in particular fields.

The public shows great curiosity in the mystery of this greatness. Where does it come from? What are the families of gifted individuals like? Were there special events that turned the child prodigy into a successful professional? How important was training or motivation? Social scientists need to plumb these issues in cases of undeniable talent. In so doing, as the scholars in this volume affirm, researchers may build a knowledge of human abilities and development that can inform and inspire teacher and student in many areas of human endeavor.

These chapters depict tantalizing new ways of approaching giftedness — considerations that begin to illuminate a number of the troublesome areas of ignorance that permeate our understanding, including the contributions of genetics, motivation, culture, and domain specific knowledge and abilities. The true value of these chapters must be gauged, however, by the ideas and research plans they stimulate in readers' minds and in the new empirical studies they generate. Thus, we hope that you will become our partner in this most intriguing enterprise.

Peter B. Read

**4**

## References

Clausen. J. A. (Ed.). *Socialization and Society.* Boston: Little, Brown, 1968.

McClelland, D. C., Baldwin, A. L., Bronfenbrenner, U., and Strodtbeck, F. L. (Eds.). *Talent and Society.* New York: D. Van Nostrand, 1958.

Roedell, W. C., Jackson, N. E., and Robinson, H. B. *Gifted Young Children.* New York: Teachers College Press, 1980.

Terman, L. M. "The Discovery and Encouragement of Exceptional Talent." *American Psychologist,* 1954, *9,* 221–230.

*Peter B. Read is a staff associate at the Social Science Research Council. A sociologist, Dr. Read's interests include child development, education, social stratification, and criminology.*

# Editor's Notes

Although journals continue to publish articles about gifted children and although research on creativity test performance ploughs on, it is fair to say that current research on giftedness and creativity is moribund or at least it has run out of steam. What is needed, it seems, is to infuse the field with new life, fresh perspective or even good substantive criticism, to show that there are lively issues in the investigation of giftedness yet to be pursued. It is toward this goal of rejuvenation that the present volume is aimed.

We believe that the traditional emphasis on precocious test performance, however productive, has had an unfortunate tendency to narrow the focus of the field, leaving outside its borders many interesting research questions. As things stand now, we know a great deal about a few things and almost nothing about many others concerning giftedness. We know almost every detail imaginable about children who achieve IQ scores above 130 and below 160 on standard tests, but we know next to nothing about children with even higher scores. We know a great deal about children who score well on Guilford or Torrance tests of divergent thinking, but we know next to nothing about child prodigies. We know a great deal about administrative arrangements in the public schools intended to help gifted children (tracking, acceleration, special classes, special schools, grade skipping), but we know next to nothing about the social, cultural, or educational conditions under which extraordinary human potential in specific fields is brought to expression. There are, for example, hundreds of empirical studies reporting the effects of tracking but nary a study on the advantages and disadvantages of early musical training. We do not even know for sure if the widely assumed relationship between early cultivation of talent in music, art, mathematics, and so forth and later achievement is as strong as we think it is. Even twenty years after Getzels and Jackson called for research on the topic, we know next to nothing about the implications of choosing one definition of giftedness versus another for identification, selection, or programs for the development of talent.

As the reader will see, this volume presents little new research. Its aim is rather to set an agenda for research, theory, and practice that reflects the aim of the committee, collectively and individually, to utilize insights and findings from the developmental sciences for the better understanding of giftedness and creativity. Of these developmental sciences we principally use psychology, but you will also see biology, brain research, epistemology, and even literature brought into the discussion. Although the members of our committee are not of one mind (to say the least!), we agree on the one point that developmental approaches are the most promising ones available to stimulate and guide our work for the foreseeable future.

As our former chairman Robert Sears has pointed out, however, development can and has meant many things to many people; it is one of those words that is overused and underdefined, almost as bad as creativity in this respect. In special education it seems to refer to anything that helps, such as a developmental reading clinic. In general education, development is often used in counseling centers to mean assisting the student to become more mature and better adjusted. And I have always deplored the way the word is used in business to refer to housing projects or shopping centers, when the landscape is so often transformed into something totally unrelated to what was there before.

Rather than try to describe in detail what we as a group mean by development, I will leave readers to do this for themselves as they read the various chapters. Suffice it to say that we see development as the transformation and reorganization of a person's ways of experiencing the world, brought about through the complex interplay of the person and whatever set of internal and external forces interact to bring about change. How this process works is seen as the central problem of our inquiry. It is our hunch that cases of extreme giftedness or creativity will tell us a great deal about this process of change. And the deeper our understanding of development (in this sense), the better we will comprehend the full range of human talents and achievements. Or at least that is what we have come to believe.

Only the future will show to what degree our commitment to developmental approaches to giftedness and creativity will be fruitful; we thank the Social Science Research Council and the Andrew W. Mellon Foundation for giving us the opportunity to begin to pursue our course.

David Henry Feldman
Editor

*David Henry Feldman is associate professor,*
*Eliot-Pearson Department of Child Study, Tufts University.*

*Our knowledge of giftedness as it develops into creativity is primitive.*
*New theory and new research methods are needed. Indeed, a distinct*
*psychology of exceptional achievement is necessary.*

# On the Hypothesized Relation Between Giftedness and Creativity

*Howard E. Gruber*

There have been three main ways of studying human extraordinariness, separated by high walls. Some investigators study *giftedness*—children functioning at unusually high levels; giftedness is often equated with precocity. Others study adult creativity—either the personality of the creative adult or the process of adult creativity—focussing on indisputably outstanding individuals. A third group study supposed creative processes in ordinary individuals; these are usually experimental or quasi-experimental studies.

In this essay I undertake three tasks, all guided by the ultimate hope of someday breaking down those walls. My first task is to examine the reasons one might have for wanting to understand extraordinariness and its development. Here, I hope also to show that there are important relationships among the guiding reasons, the research methods adopted, and the problems encountered. My second task is to examine three quite different ways of framing the idea of giftedness: the person as given, the child as child, and the person as developing. Again, the choice of frame controls the research strategy that emerges. A third task is to sketch the evolving systems approach to the study of creativity that my students and I have been working on for some years. This approach serves as a framework for my insistence that we reexamine the connection between giftedness and creativity. I will argue that we know only a few

D. Feldman (Ed.). *New Directions for Child Development: Developmental Approaches to Giftedness and Creativity*, no. 17.
San Francisco: Jossey-Bass, September 1982.

adult cases reasonably well and almost nothing about the childhood origins of the most important aspects of these adults' creative work. By the same token, then, there must be a large gap in our understanding of the growth of creativity from childhood on.

## Why Study Extraordinary People?
## Why Study Extraordinary Qualities in People?

I put the question in these somewhat different ways in order to avoid prejudicing the case regarding a difficult question. Some would have it that every child is gifted and the central goal should be to discover each child's gifts and nurture them. This position is put forward in a novel way in Michael Armstrong's *Closely Observed Children* (1980). Others would have it that only some individuals have extraordinary gifts and the central goal should be to discover and nurture those few; this is the prevailing view in the gifted child movement.

For the time being, we do not need to choose between these two formulations. Indeed, making a premature choice might narrow our vision and lead to neglect of important issues. For example, if indeed every child is gifted in some way or other, to accommodate everyone there must be a large variety of gifts — that is, ways of being extraordinary. Such a conception would dictate a particular search strategy (wide search pattern, prolonged observation) in looking for the gifts that are our objects of study. If, on the other hand, our definition of giftedness is much narrower and the variety of gifts smaller, the search strategy now popular (small test battery reduced to a very small number of scores, infrequent tests) might be appropriate.

Our committee, as evidenced in its name (the Social Science Research Council Committee on Development, Giftedness, and the Learning Process), is committed to the study of the development of extraordinariness. We believe there is now enough evidence to argue confidently that extraordinary talents require long growth and much nurturing. Since this growth process is poorly understood and for the most part ignored, one of our tasks is to foster the study of extraordinary development.

We also believe that early gifts, no matter how they are evidenced, do not necessarily flower into creative achievement or creative lives. Again, the connection between giftedness and creativity is poorly understood. From a research point of view, looking only at giftedness without looking also at the adult creative process might well lead down a blind alley. A widely successful heuristic in problem solving is to reason backwards, from the characteristics of the desired solution, to the penultimate steps leading to that end state, to the steps before those penultimate steps, and so on back to some known or attainable starting point (Newell, Shaw, and Simon, 1962; Polya, 1957). If we apply this heuristic to our present tasks, it means that we must look at the mature creative process and ask what the steps are that lead up to it. (I use *creative* here in a large enough sense to accommodate all sorts of effective extraordinariness.)

Given that our chief goal is to understand extraordinary development, we need to link up the study of giftedness with the study of creativity and to study the growth of this connection in the individual.

Let us return to our starting point, and rephrase it a little. We study the development of extraordinariness because we want to know what people are like, not only in the ordinary vale of tears, a humdrum mixture of misery, fear, and small pleasures, but what they could be like, *what life could be like.* Most psychology and social science addresses itself to the typical. But our understanding of the human condition should transcend momentary reality and include a grasp of the possible. Malaria is endemic in some parts of the world: It is typical, but not normal, not optimal. In a malarial world someone must construct a vision of unheard of health. In a world of anomie and mediocre education, someone must construct a vision of people at their best. Looking at extraordinary functioning where it does occur is one way to construct that vision.

*To understand all human beings.* If we couple a hard look at the optimum with a careful examination of the differences between it and the typical, we may hope to understand the latter as well as the former. Of course, we do not mean to look only at attributes but also at conditions of life and development. This kind of scrutiny can be pursued by closely comparing the optimal with the typical. It is well illustrated in Joanna Field's *A Life of One's Own* (1952). She noticed that sometimes she was happy and other times not. She kept a diary to help her understand the difference between these two phases of her life and rediscovered a gift for experience that, as a striving professional, she had lost.

*To facilitate innovation, to foster the transformation of human existence.* Few will deny the existence of seemingly intractable social and human problems. I forbear to list them here. Few will deny the need for extraordinary talents, both to invent and to implement solutions. Not least among the problems is the thwarting of human development, so that nurturing extraordinariness is both an end in itself and a means to other ends. But to nurture one must understand.

*To improve the chances of human survival.* Again, few will deny that human beings now constitute a major threat to their own environment or that the danger of thermonuclear war poses a threat to our existence as a species. Even now there are recognized fields of endeavor that draw upon gifts relevant to these problems—the gifts of sympathy, morality, cooperativeness, altruism, commitment, love of life. If we need to think in new ways, we need to search for and focus on gifts that will lead us in new directions.

Here is an episode (as retold in the epic poem *Peace March;* Brand, 1980, p. 34) from the life a one child, Sadako Sasaki, that underlines the reason for the search:

> The crane
> according to Japanese legend
> lives a thousand years, so a paper crane
> means a wish
> for a happy, long life.
> Ten years after the atom bombing
> a twelve-year-old girl in Hiroshima,
> Sadako Sasaki, who had been exposed
> to the bomb's radiation,
> developed leukemia. A friend
> sent her a letter in the hospital,
> enclosing a paper crane.
> Sadako thought,
> If I fold a thousand cranes,
> I have to get well. She folded
> nine hundred and sixty-four and died.

Now, in Hiroshima's Peace Park there is a bronze statue of Sadako, holding over her head a crane in bronze. The paper crane has become the symbol of the Japanese peace movement.

Was Sadako Sasaki gifted? Who sculpted the crane? Who made the symbol? Was she creative?

## Conceptual Frameworks for the Idea of Giftedness

The term *gifted* has come to represent an implicit hypothesis about the adult performance of a person identified as extraordinary in childhood. The hypothesis has three parts: (1) the preformationist belief that, at some point early in life, the "die is cast," the person's potential is defined and circumstances merely dictate the degree to which the potential will be achieved, (2) the prediction that extraordinary children will become extraordinary adults, and (3) the more detailed prediction that the domain in which the child is extraordinary is a good indicator of the domain in which he or she will be extraordinary as an adult. The point chosen for fixation of the future varies. For some members of this family of approaches the die is cast at the moment of conception, for others in infancy or in early childhood, and for still others some time in adolescence. All these, taken together, may be contrasted with views that postulate a person permanently engaged in a process of self-reconstruction.

In practice, this preformationist belief system has been closely allied with psychometric approaches to measuring abilities. This alliance has often led to the identification of giftedness with the supposedly best measured ability, IQ. This set of ideas has had the unfortunate consequence that many psychologists have turned away from the study of extraordinariness because they do not like or trust the peculiar products of this by now conventional marriage of preformationist and psychometric thought.

But *homo sapiens* is an extraordinary species, and our most creative and interesting members, rather than the typical, may best represent our essential nature. Human extraordinariness is too important to be left under the sole guardianship of preformationists and psychometricians. Let us now consider three of the possible frameworks for the idea of giftedness.

**Person as Given.** In spite of the very thin evidence, there is an almost overwhelming tendency to believe that the individual maintains a constant position in a series of three parallel "scoring systems." The form of the accepted argument runs: The child's score on X is a good predictor of the adult's score on Y. In this preformationist perspective, the ideal case would look like child A or child B in Table 1.

No one would be interested in the correlation $r_{x_c y_a}$ unless he or she also believed that this measure had implications for $r_{x_a y_a}$ or, through a natural short cut, $r_{x_c y_a}$.

It is generally taken for granted that $x_c$ and $x_a$ are scores on similar tests, or tests of the same ability, simply adjusted for age. The major tests in question are constructed to produce monotonic functions in which performance improves steadily (up to some limit) as age increases. Precocity and percentile standing in comparison with one's agemates have the same measure. From this it follows that precocity in $x_c$ is regarded as the best predictor of $y_a$.

ible. Let us for the moment accept the widespread view that originality and creativity are almost the same thing, so much so that divergent thinking tests of originality are deemed good indicators of creativity. Let us combine this assumption with another, the idea that precocity in cognitive variables of the kind measured in Piagetian tasks are, as ought to be expected, well correlated with general intelligence as measured by IQ scores. Remember that Piaget deliberately chose tasks revealing universals of intellectual growth. Then, aren't we saying that rapid progress along this well-trodden path—that is, precocious achievement of widely shared ways of thinking and acting—is a good indicator of future performance in tasks requiring originality, of conduct in situations requiring departure from the generally accepted? To make the point as clear as I can, I will recast it as a series of propositions.

### Table 1. Four Developmental Pathways

| | Test X | | Test Y |
| Individual | $X_c$ (Child) | $X_a$ (Adult) | $Y_a$ (Adult) |
|---|---|---|---|
| A | high | high | high |
| B | average | average | average |
| C | high | high | average |
| D | average | average | high |

*Argument 1.*

Proposition 1. Precocity means rapid progress in conventionally recognized, valued, and widely achieved cognitive skills.

Proposition 2. Rapid progress in developing these conventional skills leads to later success in creative work.

Proposition 3. Childhood precocity can be used to predict adult creativity.

*Argument 2.*

Proposition 4. Creativity entails doing something new.

Proposition 5. Originality is essential to creativity.

Proposition 6. Measures of originality are predictive of creative achievement.

Argument 1 and Argument 2 combine to produce

Proposition 7. Precocity in conventional cognitive skills can be used to predict adult creative achievement.

Why not expect just the opposite of propositions 3 and 7? The child who hangs back in going down the universal path may be just the one who keeps his or her eye fresh for new views of the world. Then the relevant picture might look like child D in Table 1. But this is an odd way of looking at matters. Is there any evidence that gives it some credibility? Yes:

Artists must be able to suppress or avoid the normal perceptual constancies. For the ordinary business of living we must see the far off man as six-feet tall, the saucer on the table as circular, the piece of coal in the sunlight as black. The artist, however, must be able to see far off objects as smaller, the saucer as oval, and the coal in the sun as bright, for that is how they must be painted to give a realistic impression (Gibson, 1966; Gombrich, 1960). Nor is there any correlation between these normal perceptions and those of artists (Gruber, 1952).

Getzels and Csikzentmihalyi (1976) found a *negative* correlation between divergent thinking scores of art students and their creative success in the art world some five years later.

Numerous investigators have failed to find a large correlation between measures of intelligence.

Albert Einstein as an adult obviously had a very special way of looking at the world; as a child, far from being precocious, he was slow to speak and unsuccessful in school.

I grant freely this is not an ironclad case; other evidence could be cited supporting the conventional picture of the relation between early giftedness and later creativity. But not very much. I wish only to propose that unconventional views, such as those just discussed, are not entirely implausible. It should, moreover, be recalled that Piaget, on grounds different from those I have cited, mounted a powerful attack on the preformationist point of view entailed in the acceptance of the child as given.

*Child as Child.* There is an almost overwhelming tendency to discuss giftedness in relation to the future of the child rather than the present: Who will she *become?* Will he succeed? Will she be truly great?

But it is possible to imagine a different perspective. The gifted child might be the one who, as a child, most enjoys himself or the one who most entertains us. Or she might be the one who is most helpful now. Or the one who can make the most wonderful art now, even though we know, from Gardner's work, that this gift will almost inevitably fade (Gardner, 1980).

Most of us do not get much pleasure out of contemplating measurements for their own sake, but someone who did might call that child gifted who now displays an enjoyable measure of height or a pleasing intelligence test score.

There are, then, experiential, utilitarian, and aesthetic perspectives that might orient us without our stepping out of the present. But no, we are all thoroughly committed to those meanings of giftedness that have implications for the future, for the adult to come.

The most striking exception to this tendency that I know of is Michael Armstrong's work (1978, 1980). Watching each child in a school over many months, he sees one as a philosopher, one as a poet, one as an artist—each seriously engaged in a special pursuit, often quite unobtrusively. Since each is special, only a few would be caught in the net of a testing procedure fishing for giftedness on a few standard dimensions. Armstrong makes no claim about the future performance of these children. He tells us only that if we want to see how each child is special, we must watch patiently and closely.

I do not know how to deal with this thesis in the present context. My own research commitment has been to the study of adult creativity in unique cases; our shared theoretical equipment focuses mainly on cognitive universals. The specialness of a child seems to fall through our net. And yet, when we speak of adult creativity, the phrase *a sense of specialness* will not be strange to us. For the present I can only leave it as a question, but one to remember: How do we deal with this quality we prize, specialness?

***Person as Developing Through Continuous Interaction of Organism and Environment.*** At a sufficient level of abstraction, everyone claims to be an *interactionist,* agreeing that nature and nurture both contribute to development. But certain genetic factors seem so visible that, in practice, a theoretical interactionism often turns into a quasi-hereditarian point of view. It is asserted, for example, that hereditary differences account for most of the variance in some psychological variable, usually IQ. This position has come in for its share of criticism (to which I have contributed). But when we look at extraordinary children, their performance often seems so magical that the appreciative observer may relapse into quasi-hereditarianism. From a developmental perspective, this is most unfortunate: The observer is deprived of the keen vision needed to see the environment at work and deprived also of the lively imagination necessary to guide reconstruction of the environment in favorable ways. It is perhaps only a minor irony that, as far as psychology goes, the genes influencing intelligence and creativity are completely unidentified. Evidence for them is entirely circumstantial and statistical. In contrast, we can practically see the environment at work: On one side, the dark Satanic mills, on the other, the master working with her apprentice, the father playing with his baby.

This issue is so important to a developmental perspective on any human attribute that it is worth dwelling on here.

Everyone knows that the genetic make-up transmitted from generation to generation has a profound effect on development. No environmental manipulation will turn an infant chimpanzee into a human being nor a fox into a lynx. These are hard facts of biological science. Compared to these, claims of environmental effects on the course of development seem pale psychological speculations or wishful thinking. But let us look at some clear cases.

*A queen bee and a worker bee are genetically indistinguishable.* But they are profoundly different in form and in their function in the hive. The queen is longer and more slender, does little but mate and lay eggs. As a grub she and she alone eats the "royal jelly" provided for her by the worker bees. And it is this special feeding that makes all the difference between the one queen in the hive and her sisters, numbering thousands of workers.

Or to take an even more dramatic example, in the marine worm, *Bonellia viridis,* any young individual reared from an isolated egg becomes a female. But "if newly hatched worms were released in water containing females... some of the young worms were attracted to the females and became attached to the female proboscis. These were transformed into the males and eventually migrated to the female reproductive tract where they became parasitic" (Gardner, 1972, pp. 143–144; see also Dobzhansky, 1955). Thus, this environmental difference turned the course of development so that one individual became a large female, the other a tiny male living inside the female.

The dramatic effects of environment on development are found everywhere in the living world. They are hard biological facts, just as our knowledge of genetic transmission is, and indeed, they are as much a part of the science of genetics. There are different ways of understanding the interaction of heredity and environment; although we cannot go further into that complex subject here, it should be said that any simple solution is sure to be simpleminded.

On the side of mental retardation, there seem to be some clear and known cases of specifiable genetic mechanisms controlling the development of intelligence. One of the best known is phenylketonuria (PKU), a metabolic deficiency leading to severe idiocy and early death. But the genetic defect producing PKU is now known to be not a "gene for stupidity" but an inability of the child to avoid poisoning himself or herself with his or her own metabolites. When dietary compensations for the metabolic defect are made, the child develops normally. Something similar can be said for a number of other known conditions.

When we turn back to the topic of giftedness and creativity, we find absolutely no hard knowledge that imposes on us the intellectual necessity of believing either that the gifted are extraordinary because of superior genetic endowment, or that they are extraordinary because of some unusual treatment bestowed on them, such as that received by the queen bee. Insisting on one or the other conclusion or on some vague compromise is useless and confusing. We need to find another road for our thinking.

## Two Research Strategies for Relating Giftedness and Creativity

*Tracking the Process of Development.* In the long run, we would like to know exactly how every human being develops potential through his or her own thought and action in the world. We would like to be able to trace the steps of development and to understand the choices making up a particular developmental pathway and thus characterizing any person's life. We would like to know how very specific environmental events affect the course of development. Like embryologists, then, we would like to know how some people synthesize themselves in a long series of steps, through their activity in an everchanging environment. Then would we know:

| | |
|---|---|
| how a gifted child | becomes a creative adult? |
| how a gifted child | becomes an ordinary mortal? |
| how an ungifted child | becomes a creative adult? |
| how an ungifted child | becomes an ordinary mortal? |

It pains me to write the words *ungifted child.* Polite convention usually leaves this part of our professional jargon implicit, a case of silent euphony. Maybe it is worth the pain in exchange for the pleasure of making visible the sequence "an ungifted child becomes a creative adult." Piaget tells us that those who have achieved the stage of formal operations complete their tables of possibilities, and so should we.

We are very far from the advanced state of knowledge necessary to understand developmental pathways. We have a long row to hoe. Rather than starting at the beginning, we might apply the honorable heuristic of starting at the desired end state and working our way backward to whatever initial conditions existed.

*Starting with Known Creators.* If we want to know how people become extraordinary adults, we can start with some of the latter, find out how they do whatever it is that we find extraordinary about them, and then try to find out how they came to do it. If we could understand the transformation of an adolescent into a creative adult we might then pursue the understanding of a child becoming an adolescent on the road to creativity. If we could understand an adult who has led a creative life, we might then work backwards to ask how this promising young adult organized his or her life as a whole so as to remain a self-actualizing, creative person.

At this stage of our work, we are not yet ready to trace the whole course of creative lives. But we can say a great deal about creative work, within a developmental framework. That will be the subject of the last part of this chapter.

## Some Problems in the Study of the Development of Giftedness and Creativity

The problems facing us in the future study of the development of giftedness and creativity may be grouped under seven major headings, each a whole research domain.

The first problem is our incomplete knowledge of development. Our knowledge is incomplete in at least three fundamental ways.

*Stages of the Life Cycle.* We are only beginning to look at intellectual growth in late adolescence and early adulthood. In early April 1981, there was for the first time a national symposium on investigators of postformal operations (Commons, 1981). This grew out of the recognition that the attainment of formal operations, described by Inhelder and Piaget (1958) as being achieved in early adolescence, is by no means sufficient for describing high level adult thinking and creativity. Thus, in spite of the enormous upsurge of developmental research in the last twenty-five years, we do not have a complete picture of normal development. By the same token, we are ignorant of supernormal or extraordinary developments beyond early adolescence. In other words, at just that point in the life cycle where whatever we might mean by early giftedness must be transformed into effective extraordinariness, our knowledge runs out. Something similar could be said for all the later stages of creative lives (Gruber and Voneche, 1976).

*Unilinear Theories of Development.* Virtually all theories of development (Piaget, Erikson, Freud) are unilinear (Gruber and Voneche, 1977). In other words, each describes a single developmental pathway, a set of stages in which A prepares the way for B prepares the way for C and so forth. But if we are interested in unique or unusual gifts, how do we know that these fit neatly into schemata provided by unilinear theories? Embryological theories deal with differentiating structures; evolutionary theories deal with the branching system of nature. In just this area of giftedness and creativity, where we are concerned with innovation, differentiation, and the remarkable, how can we base our understanding on a unilinear theory of the repetitive, predictable, and unremarkable?

*Focus of Research Limited to Universals.* One of Piaget's great achievements was to help psychology free itself from the trivial and the nonsensical by studying the intellectual development of profound and essential universals that had formerly been the province of philosophers: the child's ideas of object, space, time, causality, number, chance, and motion. This concern for universals properly characterizes almost all research on intellectual development. But if we are interested in the extraordinary, this knowledge must be linked up with new knowledge about the development of that which is not universal, that which is remarkable, unique (Feldman, 1980).

The topic of conservation provides an example. We know that babies during the first eighteen months develop and perfect their idea of the permanent object. In the period of concrete operations children, untaught, develop the ability to handle increasingly complex aspects of the conservation of matter under the transformation of shape (Piaget and Inhelder, 1969; Piaget and Szeminska, 1952). The adolescent or young adult will later be taught to use particular conservation principles to solve standard science problems. I have observed that, beyond that point, professional scientists often use the abstract idea of conservation principles to restructure a problem. Faced with the task of inventing an explanation for a known phenomenon, the physicist asks himself or herself, "What quantity is conserved in this situation?" and searches a repertoire of natural invariants for an appropriate approach to the problem. Beyond this, a creative achievement occurs when the scientist uses a similar strategy to guide the process of discovery. William Harvey, for example, measured the rate of flow of blood past a central point in the circulatory system, found that the total amount passing the point per hour far outweighed the total weight of the body. From this he reasoned that the body could not be producing so much blood every hour; consequently there must be a return route, and the blood must circulate in a closed loop (Harvey, 1963).

Thus he used an idea about the conservation of weight to guide a physiological inquiry. But we have no reason at all to believe that precocity in attaining conservation was important in such a life as Harvey's. Keeping alive the capacity to wonder, to ask strange questions about ordinary things when other children have settled matters and laid them to rest — this may well be the way to creativity. We need to understand the emergence of uniqueness and the relation between the unique and the universal. It may be the case, but we do not actually know it, that precocity in the attainment of these universals presages a life of creative achievement. But it is not unreasonable to ask, whether children who resist movement along the universal pathways — that is, are not precocious — include some who are most likely to see the world in a new way, or do or say something extraordinary. We do not know that precocity in universals portends extraordinariness in nonuniversals.

In other words, as we modify or reject psychometric traditions by introducing recent developmental thought, we should not make the mistake of confusing the typical with the optimal or precocity with originality.

The second problem is our *embryonic knowledge of creativity*. This is a vast subject and I will restrict myself to two points.

*Failure of Psychometric Approach.* There was, for about two decades, an enormous investment of research energy into tests of *divergent thinking*. There is hardly a shred of evidence that scores on such tests correlate with real creative performance in any line of human endeavor (Barron and Harrington, 1981). Indeed, there are very few validation studies that actually correlate test performance with real creative achievement (Fox, 1981). One recent study (Getzels and Csikszentmihalyi, 1976) found a negative correlation between divergent thinking scores and later success as an artist.

*Paucity of Case Studies.* There are very few case studies of the way creative people actually do their work. Charles Darwin is probably the best studied scientist, but even his work and life are very incompletely examined in spite of a wealth of available documentation (Gruber, 1981a). In particular, the period of his life representing the transition from adolescence to young adulthood has hardly been written about at all (Gruber, in press; Vidal, in press). Perhaps Newton and Freud have been studied almost as much as Darwin, but after that the thread of knowledge soon runs out. We have a great deal of piecemeal, sketchy knowledge about creative people. Even excellent intellectual biographies are simply not detailed or searching enough to give us a picture of the creative person at work. It should be said that there is now a small but strong undercurrent of interest in doing this kind of research.

The third problem is to correct our ideas of giftedness and creativity with *studies of prolonged training.* In the area of training of prodigies, Feldman (1980) has made a good beginning. With regard to specialized training of the kind studied by experimental psychologists interested in attention, memory, formal operations, there is a small but important group of studies by Ericcson, Chase, and Faloon (1980), Kuhn and Ho (1980), Spelke, Hirst, and Neisser (1976), and others. When the goal of an experiment is optimization rather than measurement of the typical, remarkable things can happen. In Ericcson's study, for example, an ordinary college student reached the level of performance of a mnemonics expert (memory wizard) after only 200 hours of training. If something similar could be done with the same person for two or three cognitive skills and then for their intercombinations, we have no idea what might result.

The fourth problem is that *psychometric studies of giftedness have traditionally centered on IQ scores.* What little we know suggests that there may be no strong relation between very high IQ and creative achievement (see, for example, Getzels and Jackson, 1962). Yet the major study of giftedness, Terman's, is centered around the concept of IQ. We have no tests that can discriminate between the Titans and their team members and no tests that can predict creative lives from early high scores (sometimes called giftedness).

The fifth problem is *the tuning problem.* When is a gift a gift? We slip easily into thinking that high achievement in science or the arts is what we need, what we mean by creativity. But is this the case? Today's gifted children must solve tomorrow's problems. American society has learned how to produce large numbers, probably large enough for social needs, of scientists and engineers. We, and our counterparts in other advanced nations, know how to create technological innovation. We are smart, but are we wise? If what is needed for the future are wise and compassionate people who will know what to do to preserve our species and make a better life, then shouldn't we search for ways of identifying and nurturing the gifts of wisdom and compassion? The psychometric and the Piagetian traditions share a one-sided emphasis on quasi-scientific intellectual attainments. Feldman (1980) has advanced the idea that creativity occurs when gifts are tuned to promising tasks. (Isaac Newton in the stone age would not have been gifted, nor the conductor Toscanini in a completely individualistic society.) From a practical point of view we are oriented toward the present and the future; but our research must be based on the present and the past. A thoroughgoing approach to the development of giftedness and creativity must deal with these questions of the interaction of person and world, of the place of the person in history.

The sixth problem is *the intimacy problem*. What shall be the standards for governing our search for the extraordinary? Suppose we have a list of seven good things: A person is gifted if he or she has a lot of GT's 1–7. Along comes someone with not too much of GT's 1–7 but a fantastic amount of 8. If we are only watching out for GT's 1–7, we may never notice this outlier. But the remedy does not rest with adding 8 to our list. The observer must be a person of great breadth who will notice something extraordinary whether it be 8 or $8^{8^8}$. And breadth is not enough: The observer must be watching when the extraordinary thing happens. The psychometric ethos and the overcrowded classroom both militate against such patient observation.

The seventh problem is *the criterion problem,* studies of giftedness and creativity, which vary enormously in the level of attainment deemed unusual enough to be included in the study. Terman worked with the upper 1 percent; Lehman's study of *Age and Achievement* (1953) is based on the all-time greats. Suppose Terman and others working in that vein had actually succeeded in predicting high achievement at the one in a hundred level. What would that have told us about the one-in-a-million?

If we choose the path of raising our criterion level so that our primary interest is in very high levels of creativity (one in a million would mean a panel of 200 subjects in the United States today, certainly not all to be counted among the all-time greats), then something has to happen to our research goals. For rare events, known only after the fact, we cannot aim at finding methods of prediction and nurturance.

But we could find greatly gifted people, as evidenced by their work and lives, and study them closely. My point here is not to argue for one method of research. I wish to bring out the fact that there is a strong connection between our approach to the criterion problem and our choice of methods.

Imagine an astronomer who refuses to look at novas and supernovas because they are atypical phenomena. Or, on the other hand, imagine an astronomer who looks long and lovingly at these brilliant events in the heavens, goes to great pains to develop a special *astrophotometer* for measuring their departure from normal brightness of stars and concludes admiringly that, indeed, these stars are endowed with novoid genius. Still again, imagine a third astronomer who thinks novas are wonderful and, wanting to see more of them, recalibrates his or her instruments (to a lower criterion level) so that more bright stars will appear to them as novas.

But none of these savants would be using the brilliant phenomena of their domain for the main purpose that scientists have evolved in every field of successful inquiry—the long, patient struggle to make sense of the domain as a whole, to understand it.

To this end, unusual events may be particularly useful if they can be conceived of as magnifying or extremizing interesting processes and thereby making them easier to study. This would be the case with genetics, for decades using the fruitfly, *drosophila melanogaster,* as an experimental animal because it breeds rapidly and because it has unusual, giant chromosomes in the salivary glands that make it possible to observe quite directly various chromosomal configurations. This would also be the case with students of intellectual growth choosing children to study because processes of development are so rapid in the early years.

In another vein, unusual events may be particularly interesting if they can tell us about the origins of important phenomena. Evolutionists must be interested in mutations. But not for their own sake; this is the key point. The indispensable task is to link up these extraordinary events with the domain of inquiry as a whole, to use the novas to illuminate the heavens of inquiry.

## The Evolving Systems Approach

In the last part of this chapter, I wish to sketch briefly the evolving systems approach (Gruber, 1980) to the study of creative people and give some indication of its bearing on the understanding of development from early giftedness to adult creativity. As it stands now, this approach is the result of the collaborative efforts of a number of students and colleagues. We believe it is a new paradigm, at least in the sense of that word made popular by Thomas Kuhn (1962)—that is, a shared way of working and thinking. Whether it is to become a paradigm in the older sense of the term, a model to be followed by others, remains to be seen.

Not long after my training as an experimental psychologist in visual space perception, I first undertook the study of the history of science as a fresh approach to the psychology of thinking. I was entirely ignorant of Piaget's seminal work in that area (and equally oblivious to most of his other work). I was simply troubled that the experimental psychology of thinking dealt with processes on a short time scale—that is, experimental tasks taking a few minutes or an hour, and relied on problems provided by the experimenter, rather than on those emerging from the abiding concerns of the subject. Naturally enough, my trail soon led to Geneva, where it had already been discovered that cognitive development takes a long time.

In our work on creativity, we have avoided calling our approach developmental simply because that word suggests the study of child and adolescent development. On the other hand, our work has a distinctly developmental flavor and has been influenced by developmental theory. Unless one believes that psychological development stops at the end of puberty, a lifetime leaves plenty of room for creative growth. And that is what we study — the growth of ideas, of affect, and of purpose. To put matters as briefly as possible, in the evolving systems approach we treat the creative person as someone constituted of three loosely coupled systems, each evolving over long periods of time, throughout the life history: an organization of knowledge, an organization of affect, and an organization of purposes. Just this brief sketch indicates how far removed are our concerns from approaches that attempt to measure either intelligence or creativity as a collection of traits, for in all such literature knowledge is treated as the capacity to absorb information, rather than as a personal organization of particular cognitive structures; affect is almost invisible, and purpose hardly mentioned. It should be added, however, that there is at least one research tradition that comes close to ours, the person-centered work of Henry A. Murray and his colleagues (1981).

Our cognitive case studies aim to understand the relationships among the individual's cognitive economy as a whole, the actual contents of thought and experience involved in the creative production of a work, and the work itself. Rather than seeking inductive generalization by examining many cases, we exploit each case to bring out those processes that it displays particularly clearly: My study of Darwin thus examines the conceptual complexity and density of an argument undergoing change (Gruber, 1981a). My work in progress on Piaget emphasizes the formative years in which Piaget was developing a poetic and philosophical passion that would support his long scientific career (Gruber and Voneche, 1977). Wallace's work on Dorothy Richardson emphasizes the "fabric of experience" and the relation of the novelist's life to her work (1982). Osowski's study emphasizes the ensemble of metaphors and images of wide scope in William James' work (Gruber, 1978; Osowski, 1982). Jeffrey's study emphasizes the process of revision over some fifty years in the successive drafts of one poem by Wordsworth (1982). But aspects emphasized in one study are nevertheless present in all the others. For example, every creative person works with some ensemble of metaphors and figures of thought (Gruber, 1978; Nemerov, 1978). As the picture fills in, we hope to be able to relate these aspects in more coherent wholes. The wholes in question are not abstract generalizations across persons but whole creative individuals, each one a unique configuration.

Thus, the aim of our collaborative effort in studying several cases in very far from the inductive procedure of strengthening an argument statistically by increasing the number of observations. The case studies stand in a relation of complementarity rather than replication. We hope to bring multiple perspectives to bear on a very complex group of processes. What is learned from one case may be applied in another, not by simple extrapolation, but with (we hope) ever increasing structural acumen, always maintaining great respect for the uniqueness of each individual.

***The Organization of Purpose.*** We slowly come to understand that our cognitive case studies are largely devoted to describing a person at work in a particular social and historical context (see Braverman, 1974). In the past, in discussions of creativity much emphasis has been placed on spontaneous and unfettered imagination, on primary process and unconscious forces, on the playful and nonrational side of creative activity. Our approach may seem to fly in the face of famous accounts, such as Kekulé's dream, Poincaré's trolley car ride, or Newton's often cited remark: "I seem to have been only like a boy playing on the seashore and diverting myself in now and then finding a smooth pebble or a prettier shell than ordinary whilst the great ocean of truth lay all undiscovered before me." But such playful spontaneity becomes fruitful only when it occurs within the context of an organized network of purposes. Both the fruits of spontaneity and those of conscious voluntary activity must be assimilated into such a network if a creative product is to result. Such a network is not the creature of a moment but the form of a lifetime. Newton did speak of play, and Newton's apple story has been used to emphasize the importance of sudden involuntary insight; but Newton also said that he arrived at the idea of gravity by always thinking about it. Read carefully, his life is far more a story of persistent effort than of sudden insights (Westfall, 1980). A similar persistence is reflected in Einstein's account of the growth of the idea of special relativity, from an image of himself riding a beam of light at the age of sixteen to his great paper ten years later (Wertheimer, 1959). Insight comes to the prepared mind; the preparation, however, is not done *to* the mind but by it, in other words, by a person who purposefully guides his or her own activity, whose dreams and drudgery are both controlled by a web of abiding goals.

Sudden insights do, of course, occur, perhaps as many as one per day in a creative life. But they do not explain creativity. Rather, they pose a task for the evolving systems approach—how to link up such short term processes, occupying between one and fifty minutes, with longer processes, spanning one to fifty years (see Gruber, 1981b).

When we speak of work, what do we mean? A human activity that is organized for the purpose of contributing to some definable product or service. Under certain conditions we may speak of work as alienated. Although the criterion of purpose is still satisfied, the purposes are those of the employers rather than the workers. Indeed, the latter may never understand or even see the product of their work (Braverman, 1974).

In the creative processes, such alienation is not possible, and this fact helps to account for the fusion of work and play. Since the goal includes novelty, the product cannot be fully defined in advance; playful and exploratory activity are therefore inherent in the task. But these must be regulated and monitored by a steady purpose if they are to have productive consequences. Of course, after the fact, the creative product may be exploited by others for ends alien to the creator, an event painfully familiar to inventors and writers. But in the making, both free fantasy and repetitive labor are harnessed to the same task, orchestrated in an activity that may be called purposeful work.

In pursuing a cognitive case study, it is always tempting to believe that one is studying the cognitive economy as a whole, not only as a moment in time but extended over the life history of the subject. Indeed, it is incumbent upon us to seek ways of approaching that ideal. Reality is a little more cramping. Each case study is opportune for illuminating certain issues precisely because those very matters that provide the most complete documentation are the ones that most concerned the subject too. It is through the creative person's voluntary efforts and purposeful work that the materials of the study were produced.

***Cognition and Affect in Two Creative Lives: Darwin and Piaget.*** How does it come about that the individual, using the universally shared mental operations of our species and the culturally shared knowledge of his or her own milieu, produces something unique? In what sense can the study of unique events be a part of scientific inquiry? Must we choose either to ignore that uniqueness that is the very source of their interest for us or to abandon the most central aim of science, universal truth?

I hope that these remarks will serve to introduce you to some of the problems that interest us and thus to our way of thought. Without stopping to answer the questions just now raised, I hasten on to some case material. The case study of Darwin moves in three main phases: first, the slow growth of a point of view during his university years and during the five years of the Beagle voyage; second, an intense period of theory construction, something like the solution of one group of focused problems, during the one and a half year period following the voyage; third, a long period — the rest of his life — of elaboration of the solution found and expansion of the point of view that permitted him to find it.

Darwin's thought is characterized neither as one great moment of insight nor as an uneventful process of monotonic, gradual change. Rather, his many insights — literally thousands — are the expression of the functioning of a system, moments of qualitative change in a continuous process of structural growth.

While this account in entirely cognitive, it is by no means devoid of feeling. We can equally well say it is entirely affective. Darwin's feelings about god or a godless world, about nature, humanity, and himself permeate his thoughts. The recognition of the kinship of homo sapiens and other animals is as much a matter of self-discovery and acceptance as it is the growth of a scientific conception of evolution.

Darwin's thought and the social context in which it occurred reveal many interesting examples of the interpenetration of individual and social processes. Most dramatic among these was the recognition that his evolutionary views were inseparable from a materialistic view of all biological and mental phenomena. Evolution was an idea dangerous enough; materialism compounded the felony. Darwin concealed his philosophical views throughout his life, and wrote publicly *sub speciae positivismus*. The psychology of affectivity cannot ignore the deep conflicts that this intellectual pattern must produce.

The psychology of cognition cannot ignore the regulative function of these general ideas and images, private and suppressed though they often be.

When we turn to Piaget, an entirely different pattern is exhibited. Far from suppressing his philosophical convictions, Piaget embraces them, flaunts them, uses them as the point of departure and the port of return for all his work.

*Networks of Enterprises.* To examine the working life of an intellectual systematically, we need a few descriptive tools that permit us to capture his or her efforts as a whole. We have found it useful to describe each life as a network of enterprises. Ferrara (1982) has elaborated a technique for describing quite different lives in this way. An enterprise is an enduring set of related tasks and problems. At a given moment, the individual prosecutes the enterprise by carrying out some of these tasks, but if he or she were ever to exhaust the set he or she would not abandon the enterprise but would invent new tasks in order to continue it, just as any entrepreneur takes steps to maintain his or her inventory. In reality, this problem seldom arises, because, within an enterprise, new tasks appear before old ones are completed. Thus, any purposeful activity has membership in one or perhaps several enterprises.

It would not be hard to describe Piaget's life in these terms. The names of some of the enterprises are as familiar to us as the great disciplines of human intellectual activity: biology, philosophy, psychology, education. These divide in interesting ways. Thus, Piaget's pursuit of philosophy can be subdivided into epistemology, logic, and ethics in such a way as to absorb ontological and metaphysical problems without attacking them frontally. Certain themes and enterprises appear early in his life and continue throughout. For example, *equilibration* and *interdisciplinarity* are dealt with in his 1918 philosophical novel, *Recherche.* The nature of formal thought is the topic of early experimental papers of the 1920s and reappears two decades later. The problem of causality is attacked vigorously in two great periods of his life, the 1920s and the 1960s, with much reflective work going on during the intervening years. The study of molluscs, begun in boyhood, continued throughout his life to be a point of departure for examination and reexamination of the relation between organism and milieu. There are numerous other examples (for a survey of this work, see Gruber and Voneche, 1977).

Having said this much, it is inviting to stop here and leave our characterization of Piaget's life as an organized network of mutually supporting enterprises with certain recurrent themes. But we may ask a further question: Is there not some underlying motive or unifying *leitmotif* that would add coherence and direction to the whole? I believe there is and that it is most clearly revealed in a little known work Piaget published in 1916, at age twenty, during the height of World War I—the prose poem, *La Mission de l'Idée* (The Mission of the Idea) (Piaget, 1916; translation in Gruber and Voneche, 1977).

The world knows Piaget as the cool epistemologist, the builder of logical structures, pursuing the difficult task of mapping children's thought onto those structures. Here we see another Piaget. He is twenty years old, already a scientist with world standing in the field of malacology. Presumably, he has been practicing formal operational thought for some years. But we do not see him rushing directly into the world to begin the long struggle toward formalization for which we know him.

Instead, we see him in the full flood of the romance of youth, writing a long prose poem, a hymn to Christian socialism, a celebration of the search for truth, a love song to the Idea. The opening verse and a fragment from the closing give the flavor of the work (Gruber and Voneche, 1977, p. 27, p. 37):

I

The Idea surges from the depths of our being. The Idea over-throws kings and priests, raises the masses, decides the outcome of battles, guides the whole of humanity. Everything is Idea, comes from the Idea, returns to the Idea. The Idea is an organism, is born, grows, and dies like organisms, renews itself ceaselessly. In the beginning was the Idea, say the mysterious words of the Christian cosmogeny...

XLVI

When the idea is reborn, every man now suffering in the sha-dows will find his place in the vast harmony which by its crescendo will make life grow, so high that it will see God. But the rebirth of the idea requires the help of everyone. Metaphysics is not an aristocratic art. The scientist, who finds hypotheses, must build over them a grand edifice that can contain them; the Christian, who in the depths of his heart has felt a life, must assimilate it by an interpretation which justifies it; the moral man, who wants a rule of conduct to govern his life, must construct an idea and from these ideas, numerous as the cells, the true idea will come forth like the soul from the body.

The poem exhibits a cathexis with nature capable of sustaining a life-time of intellectual work. It contains two powerful images of wide scope: the Idea itself, and the Lonely Traveler searching for it.

Here is affectivity, aesthetic feeling, motivation, and purpose formed into one powerful dynamo that will energize sixty years of mental strife.

Nor is this an isolated act, a momentary meandering from the straight path of science. Rather, as Piaget's life work shows, it is a fundamental preoccupation, a theme that surfaces often in his descriptions of children and from time to time takes on the more general philosophic form of explicit reflec-tion. If we want a name for this enterprise, we might call it nourishing the pas-sion of the search for truth.

If we ask how Piaget's cognitive system was organized so that it could do so much for so long, surely a large part of the answer must be that he formed a network of purposes so large and so complex that it could never come to rest.

Success in one part engendered new problems and new opportunities elsewhere in the system.

## Conclusion

If we understood how a given system came to be we would have explained, for that person, the development of early gifts into later creativity. At present, we can describe reasonably well the development of a creative person from adolescence onward. But the early shaping of a creative life remains largely terra incognita. We know next to nothing about networks of enterprise in childhood and adolescence. The knowledge and belief systems of creative adolescence are given short shrift as "juvenilia," and consequently we have almost no picture of the evolution of the system of knowledge and belief between childhood and adulthood.

If we look more closely at the interweaving of cognition, affect, and purpose in creative lives we may in time learn something of how early gifts evolve into later creativity. Albert Einstein represents a marvellous lifetime organization of the gifts of intelligence, passion, and compassion — whose interdependence has been an arrière pensée throughout this essay. Einstein said of himself: "I have no special gift — I am only passionately curious. Thus it is not a question of heredity" (Hoffman and Dukas, 1972, p. 7).

In this he was probably right. Hoffman, one of his biographers, himself a theoretical physicist and colleague of Einstein's wrote, "But talent is no great rarity, and by professional standards Einstein's scientific talent and technical skill were not spectacular. They were surpassed by those of many a competent practitioner (Hoffman and Dukas, 1972, p. 7).

Of curiosity and its fate, Einstein wrote: "It is, in fact, nothing short of a miracle that modern methods of instruction have not yet entirely strangled the holy curiosity of inquiry; for this delicate little plant, aside from stimulation, stands mainly in need of freedom; without this it goes to wreck and ruin without fail. It is a very grave mistake to think that the enjoyment of seeing and searching can be promoted by means of coercion and a sense of duty" (Einstein, 1949, p. 17).

But there is more to a man like Einstein than talent and curiosity. The same concern for unifying principles, underlying his thinking about the physical universe, dominated his social thought. He was a lifelong pacifist, and he saw this position as intimately connected with the nature of scientific thought. He wrote: "[Scientists] are inclined, by the universal character of the subject dealt with and by the necessity of internationally organized cooperation, towards an international mentality predisposing them to favor pacifist objectives" (Frank, 1948, p. 191).

If gifts must be tuned to the historical needs of their owners in order to flower into creative achievement, then it is clear that in the next few decades mere intelligence will not be enough. To survive, *Homo sapiens,* the intelligent ape, must now evolve into a creature of deeper humanity and wisdom, *Homo pacificus*. Do we know how to find and nourish that gift?

## References

Armstrong, M. "Writers, Artists, and Philosphers: Thought and Action in a Primary School Classroom." *Outlook* (Journal of the Mountain View Center for Environmental Education, University of Colorado), 1978, *27*, 3–45.

Armstrong, M. *Closely Observed Children: The Diary of a Primary Classroom.* London: Writers and Readers, 1980.

Arnheim, R. *The Genesis of a Painting: Picasso's Guernica.* Berkeley: University of California Press, 1962.

Barron, F., and Harrington, D. M. "Creativity, Intelligence, and Personality." *Annual Review of Psychology,* 1981, *32*, 439–476.

Brand, M. *Peace March, Nagasaki to Hiroshima.* Woodstock, Vt.: Countryman Press, 1980.

Braverman, H. *Labor and Monopoly Capital: The Degradation of Work in the Twentieth Century.* New York: Monthly Review Press, 1974.

Commons, M. Symposium on Postformal Operations held at Harvard University, March 1981.

Dines, A. M. *Honeybees from Close Up.* New York: Crowell, 1968.

Dobzhansky, T. *Evolution, Genetics, and Man.* New York: Wiley, 1955.

Einstein, A. "Autobiographical Notes." In P. A. Schilpp (Ed.), *Albert Einstein, Philosopher-Scientist.* New York: Harper & Row, 1949.

Ericsson, K. A., Chase, W. G., and Faloon, S. "Acquisition of a Memory Skill." *Science,* 1980, *208*, 1181–1182.

Feldman, D. H. *Beyond Universals in Cognitive Development.* Norwood, N.J.: Ablex, 1980.

Ferrara, N. A. "Networks of Enterprises: The Organization of Purpose in Creative Lives." Unpublished doctoral dissertation, Institute for Cognitive Studies, Rutgers University, 1982.

Field, J. *A Life of One's Own.* Harmondsworth, England: Pelican, 1952.

Fox, L. H. "Identification of the Academically Gifted." *American Psychologist,* 1981, *36*, 1103–1111.

Frank, P. *Einstein, His Life and Times.* London: Cape, 1948.

Gardner, E. J. *Principles of Genetics.* (4th ed.) New York: Wiley, 1972.

Gardner, H. *Artful Scribbles: The Significance of Children's Drawings.* New York: Basic Books, 1980.

Getzels, J. W., and Csikszentmihalyi, M. *Creative Vision: A Longitudinal Study of Problem Finding in Art.* New York: Wiley, 1976.

Getzels, J. W., and Jackson, P. W. *Creativity and Intelligence: Explorations with Gifted Students.* New York: Wiley, 1962.

Gibson, J. J. *The Senses Considered as Perceptual Systems.* Boston: Houghton Mifflin, 1966.

Gombrich, E. H. *Art and Illusion: A Study in the Psychology of Pictorial Representation.* New York: Pantheon, 1960.

Gruber, H. E. "The Lack of Correlation Between Objective and Perspective Size Judgment." Paper presented at Eastern Psychological Association. New York: April 1952.

Gruber, H. E. "Darwin's 'Tree of Nature' and Other Images of Wide Scope." In J. Wechsler (Ed.), *On Aesthetics in Science.* Cambridge, Mass: M.I.T. Press, 1978.

Gruber, H. E. "The Evolving Systems Approach to Creativity." In S. Modgil and C. Modgil (Eds.), *Toward a Theory of Psychological Development.* Windsor, England: NFER, 1980.

Gruber, H. E. *Darwin on Man: A Psychological Study of Scientific Creativity.* (2nd ed.) Chicago: University of Chicago Press, 1981a.

Gruber, H. E. "On the Relation Between 'Aha! Experiences' and the Construction of Ideas." *History of Science*, 1981b, *19*, 41–59.

Gruber, H. E. "The Emergence of a Sense of Purpose: A Cognitive Case Study of Young Darwin." In M. L. Commons (Ed.), *Beyond Formal Operations: Late Adolescent and Adult Cognitive Development*. New York: Praeger, in press.

Gruber, H. E., and Voneche, J. J. "Reflexions sur les opérations formelles de la pensée." ("Reflections on Formal Operations.") *Archives of Psychology*, 1976, *44*, 45–55.

Gruber, H. E., and Voneche, J. J. *The Essential Piaget*. New York: Basic Books, 1977.

Harvey, W. *The Circulation of the Blood and Other Writings*. New York: Dutton, 1963.

Hoffman, B., and Dukas, H. *Albert Einstein, Creator and Rebel*. New York: Viking, 1972.

Inhelder, B. and Piaget, J. *The Growth of Logical Thinking from Childhood to Adolescence*. New York: Basic Books, 1958.

Jeffrey, L. *Wordsworth: A Study of the Thinker as Poet*. Unpublished doctoral dissertation, Institute for Cognitive Studies, Rutgers University, 1982.

Kuhn, D., and Ho, V. "Self-Directed Activity and Cognitive Development." *Journal of Applied Developmental Psychology*, 1980, *1*, 119–133.

Kuhn, T. S. *The Structure of Scientific Revolutions*. Chicago: University of Chicago Press, 1962.

Krueger, M. L. (Ed.). *On Being Gifted*. New York: Walker, 1978.

Lehman, H. C. *Age and Achievement*. Princeton: Princeton University Press, 1953.

Murray, H. A. *Endeavors in Psychology: Selections from the Personology of Henry A. Murray*. New York: Harper & Row, 1981.

Nemerov, H. *Figures of Thought: Speculations on the Meaning of Poetry and Other Essays*. Boston: Godine, 1978.

Newell, A. , Shaw, J. C., and Simon, H. A. "The Processes of Creative Thinking." In H. E. Gruber, G. Terrell, and M. Wertheimer (Eds.), *Contemporary Approaches to Creative Thinking*. New York: Atherton Press, 1962.

Newell, A., and Simon, H. A. *Human Problem Solving*. Englewood Cliffs, N. J.: Prentice-Hall, 1972.

Osowski, J. "Metaphor as Conceptual Representation: The Organization of Experience in the Psychology of William James." Unpublished doctoral dissertation, Institute for Cognitive Studies, Rutgers University, 1982.

Pascual Leone, J. "Growing into Human Maturity: Toward a Meta-Subjective Theory of Adult Stages." In M. L. Commons (Ed.), *Beyond Formal Operations: Late Adolescent and Adult Cognitive Development*. New York: Praeger, in press.

Piaget, J. *La Mission de l'Idée. (The Mission of the Idea.)* Lausanne, Switzerland: Edition de la Concorde, 1916.

Piaget, J. *Recherche*. Lausanne: Edition de la Concorde, 1918.

Piaget, J. "The Mission of the Idea." Trans. by H. Gruber and J. J. Voneche. In H. E. Gruber and J. J. Voneche (Eds.), *The Essential Piaget*. New York: Basic Books, 1977.

Piaget, J., and Inhelder, B. *The Psychology of the Child*. New York: Basic Books, 1969.

Piaget, J., and Inhelder, B. *Le Développement des quantités physiques chez l'enfant. (The Development of the Child's Ideas of Physical Quantity.)* Neuchatel, Switzerland: Delachaux et Niestlé, 1971.

Piaget, J., and Szeminska, A. *The Child's Conception of Number*. New York: Humanities Press, 1952.

Polya, G. *How to Solve It*. Princeton: Princeton University Press, 1957.

Spelke, E., Hirst, W., and Neisser, U. "Skills of Divided Attention." *Cognition*, 1976, *4*, 215–230.

Vidal, F. "The Development of Piaget's Cognitive Processes: A Case Study in Adult Cognitive Development." In M. L. Commons (Ed.), *Beyond Formal Operations: Late Adolescent and Adult Cognitive Development*. New York: Praeger, in press.

29

Wallace, D. B. "The Fabric of Experience: A Psychological Study of Dorothy Richardson's *Pilgrimage*." Unpublished doctoral dissertation, Institute for Cognitive Studies, Rutgers University, 1982.
Weaver, W. "Probability, Rarity, Interest, and Surprise." *Scientific Monthly,* 1948, *67,* 390–392.
Wertheimer, M. *Productive Thinking.* (Rev. ed.) New York: Harper, 1959.
Westfall, R. S. "Newton's Marvellous Years of Discovery and Their Aftermath: Myth Versus Manuscript." *Isis,* 1980, *71,* 109–121.

*Howard E. Gruber is Distinguished Professor of Psychology and Director, Institute for Cognitive Studies, at Rutgers University in Newark, New Jersey. His interests include single case methods for studying exceptional cognitive development, Piagetian approaches to the study of creativity, and the psychology of Charles Darwin and and of Jean Piaget.*

*By extending and transforming certain Piagetian ideas about development, it is possible to construct a coherent framework for research on creativity, giftedness, and genius.*

# A Developmental Framework for Research with Gifted Children

*David Henry Feldman*

There has been a revolution in psychology, a revolution that has changed the way we think about intelligence and its development. This revolution is usually identified with the monumental contributions of Jean Piaget and his colleagues at the University of Geneva (see Cowan, 1978; Flavell, 1963; or Gardner, 1972, for summaries). It will be my purpose in this chapter to examine the ideas of Piaget and others who have studied general intellectual development for suggestions about how to reconceptualize research on two more specific aspects of human behavior, giftedness and creativity. As part of this process, it will be necessary to depart from some traditional ways of describing intellectual development, modifying the Piagetian framework to better accommodate the specific problems of giftedness and creativity.

Until now research on giftedness has almost exclusively come out of the psychometric tradition, where the focus has been on studying how and why gifted individuals are different from other people. Within the psychometric tradition giftedness has generally been considered synonymous with high IQ. Intelligence (and creativity as well) is seen as a quantity that is essentially

This chapter was prepared with the help of a grant from the Spencer Foundation, H. Thomas James, President. Lynn T. Goldsmith of M.I.T. and Peter B. Read of the Social Science Research Council provided helpful suggestions and comments on earlier drafts.

D. Feldman (Ed.). *New Directions for Child Development: Developmental Approaches to Giftedness and Creativity,* no. 17. San Francisco: Jossey-Bass, September 1982.

stable from infancy: It is primarily biological, a matter of heredity. Whether or not an individual realizes his or her underlying intellectual potential is a societal issue, but little can be done to modify the basic equipment. (In the early 1960s some argued that IQ was not quite so fixed as originally proposed but this optimism did not last very long or change in any fundamental way the hereditarian assumptions of the psychometric movement [Feldman, 1979b, 1980a; Jensen, 1969; Scarr and Weinberg, 1976].) Because intelligence is viewed as a stable underlying trait, the amount of ability one possesses can be measured, and this measure should predict later performance as well as measure present intelligence. In fact, a major task for researchers of giftedness appears to have been essentially predictive — to identify those children who would perform at high levels some time down the road. To be labeled gifted or creative in the psychometric manner, then, was to be given a promissory note. It is partly because the predictions of future performance based on IQ were overly optimistic — more was promised than delivered — that there is now a need for alternative ways of looking at giftedness, if not at intelligence in general (Feldman, 1977, 1979a, 1979b, 1980a).

Enough evidence has now been accumulated to know pretty well what is predicted by IQ. High IQ has predicted academic success and moderately successful careers (for men at least) in fields like business, law, medicine, the military, and academics for the well-know Terman sample (Feldman, 1979b; Sears, 1979; Terman, 1954). Extremely high IQ (above 180) has not been studied in sufficient detail to assess its value as a predictor, but preliminary results from a study of very high IQ (above 180) suggest that it conferred little additional advantage to those in the Terman group so tested, especially among the women in the sample (Feldman, in preparation). It has also become clear that IQ is not a very good predictor of original or innovative thinking, and this led during the 1950s to the design of creativity tests to do the job (Guilford, 1950). After thirty years of research, however, the ability of these tests to predict actual creativity is almost nil (Feldman, 1970, 1980a; Wallach, 1971).

The study of giftedness, perhaps the most clearly tied to the psychometric approach of all research specialties, began to fade as a major area of investigation in the 1960s. This was a time when various groups in the culture were striving for equality in all realms of social life, and testing seemed to present a barrier to the desired equal treatment. For both political and scientific reasons the study of giftedness and creativity seemed to lose its momentum (Feldman, 1977), and psychometric views were increasingly seen as scientifically uninteresting and politically unpopular. One effect of this diminished interest is that there is now an unguided quality to research in the field. And yet, perhaps because of the swing toward conservative values within the country, ambitious policies, programs, and commitments to identify and develop giftedness are increasing at what seems to be an unprecedented rate (A. Harry Passow, personal communication, 1981; Renzulli, 1980). Indeed the sense of urgency for reviving research on giftedness and creativity is heightened by the topsy-like growth of the applied field.

Thus, we are faced with a dilemma. The psychometric tradition—the bastion of creativity research—has produced two sets of instruments that, while extensively utilized by researchers, ultimately have been most disappointing in their ability to identify those talented individuals who express their abilities in highly creative and productive careers. Just as these tests have failed to fulfill their predictive promise, they have contributed little to our understanding of the emergence and development of unusual abilities.

With a growing societal commitment to the nurturance and education of gifted and talented individuals, the virtual vacuum of research concerning the development of giftedness is tragic. Clearly, previous research strategies have been impoverished. Yet we are not without the conceptual tools to generate new knowledge. Just as the methods and insights of Piaget and his colleagues revolutionized the study of cognition, so the procedures and assumptions of this approach might inspire radically different studies of giftedness.

As many readers know, Piaget's concern has been with the common, the universal in intellectal development. For this reason this theory may seem inherently unsuitable for distinguishing among individuals' unique abilities, except most broadly in terms of their overall stage of development. Indeed, one of Piaget's specific purposes was to provide an antidote to psychologists' preoccupation with the study of IQ and other measures of individual differences. Not surprisingly, the antidote seems to have taken everywhere but in the field of giftedness. Looking for ideas about giftedness from Piaget is a little like looking for ideas about God from an atheist. Yet the effort can be worthwhile in a period like this one when there seems to be a crisis in the faith.

Three key Piagetian concepts about process will guide this new look at giftedness: the notion of *interaction* between child and environment; the notion of developmental *stage*; and the notion of *transition* processes between stages. In modified form, these three notions will be central to the view of giftedness presented here. These modifications result in a developmental framework that also leads to a redefinition of creativity as an outgorwth of giftedness rather than as a separate ability (see also the chapter by Gruber in this volume). Giftedness may be considered the potential to make significant contributions to any socially valued field. This definition is quite similar to one offered by Paul Witty many years ago (Witty, 1940). If we define giftedness in this way, then we can think of creativity as the optimal use of that potential.

The problem then is to move from these broad and general definitions to more specific statements about how people achieve at high levels in various fields. The psychometric and Piagetian views both appeared to solve this problem by assuming that either IQ or formal operations is sufficient for predicting (or explaining) all levels of achievement. Questions of how an individual selects a field, masters its content, picks a specialty, and establishes a line of productive and original work were left unanswered. Yet we know that individuals who have the same IQ scores may elect (or have thrust upon them) vastly different fields to pursue and may or may not perform well within them. The same is even more true (at least in theory) for Piaget's stage of formal operations (Piaget, 1972). Since everyone is supposed to reach this stage, it is not at all clear how having achieved formal operations will distinguish among more and less gifted individuals. What is needed is a view of giftedness and creativity that is more specific and that is grounded in domains of knowledge and skill—that is, that goes beyond Piaget where necessary.

## Piaget's View of Intelligence: Interaction

Piaget has proposed that the child comes into the world with a few primitive capabilities and builds from these more and more complex systems for making sense of the world. The sequence of constructions (or stages) is a universal one, meaning that all children in all cultures over all of history have gone through the same stages in the same order. For Piaget a child is not "pre-packaged" with a given amount of intelligence but rather comes into the world with a set of tendencies to help make sense of the environment. Through encounters with the world, the child builds up representations of things and events, begins to make categories, to understand relations among people and objects, and so forth. In Piaget's view, intelligence is therefore constructed out of the child's numerous experiences; the process and general direction of development are guaranteed by biology, but each individual goes about this enormous construction project more or less autonomously (see Gardner, 1972, for a summary). The *mystery of the stages* according to Piaget (1971) is that all children construct the same stages in the same order.

For Piaget the nature of interaction in the construction of intelligence is crucial but nonspecific. Children need to live in an environment that includes objects and people, behaving in ways that objects and people do. Any more or less normal environment, however, is sufficiently rich to provide the needed *aliment* for the child's evolving mental structures (Piaget, 1971, 1972). The individual constructor is at the heart of the process; the child uses environment as he or she sees fit. (The Piagetian view shares this feature with the psychometric view.)

This laissez-faire view of the nature of the child's interaction with the environment seems inadequate in accounting for gifted performance. In studying child prodigies, for example, I have found that their extraordinary mastery of a field is the result of prolonged, systematic, and guided interaction with specific environmental forces such as teachers, peers, educational materials, technologies, competitions, and performances (Feldman, 1979a, 1980a). This would suggest that, at least for very gifted children if not for gifted people in general, specific environmental experience plays a critical role in the development of talent in various fields.

Piaget's notion of interaction, then, must be altered and extended if it is to provide a framework to guide research on giftedness. In his theory, nonspecific stimulation is sufficient for progress through the broad stages of cognitive development. Such universal changes would not, after all, be universal if they required highly specialized environments; the same laws of gravity, number, and so forth apply in the outback of Australia and in the penthouses of Manhattan. When we turn our attention to nonuniversal domains, however, a more active and specific role for environmental forces is required. Since it is unlikely that any individual will rediscover the entire developmental history of a field, the process of mastery of successive stages in a specific field is more of a joint exchange between the individual student and the accumulated wisdom of others who have greater mastery of the domain. For development to occur in any domain other than the most general ones, spontaneous environmental forces are insufficient in even the most extreme cases.

At least four sets of forces other than the individual's own talents and personal qualities affect the course of development in nonuniversal domains. First there is the field itself. As Olga Korbutt, the great gymnast once said, "If gymnastics did not exist, I would have invented it!" This quote expresses two points, really, one of which is worth noting only in passing — that is, that there seems to be a very powerful desire in extremely talented individuals, almost a compulsion, to do a certain rather specific thing. It is difficult to overestimate the power of such a drive. But it is equally true that the existence of a medium of expression that can serve as an adequate conduit for such energy is virtually never the product of a single person's efforts. And this brings us to the second point: It is the luck of the individual, for better or for worse, to be born and grow up when a particular field exists that will give form to that individual's particular talents. A field too far evolved or too little evolved may be equally mismatched to a highly pretuned talent.

Indeed, it is unlikely that Olga Korbutt would have achieved the perfection of her 1972 Olympic performance if she had not benefited from a tradition of gymnastics technique and technology from which her talents could spring. Most of the equipment, organization, standards, and procedures of gymnastics existed long before she was born; it was Olga Korbutt's good fortune to be provided with a field well enough developed to accommodate her enormous talent. So it is with any remarkable achievement. As Isaac Newton is reported to have said, "I stand on the shoulders of giants."

In addition to the existence of the field itself, there must also be exposure to the field at the proper time and in appropriate ways. If a child is "chess talented" but never sees chess played, the talent is unlikely to bloom. The more specific the talent, of course, the more crucial the right match to a domain becomes. Howard Gardner (1981), for example, wrote of the Indian mathematician Ramanujan, who was arguably the most naturally talented mathematician of this century but who was introduced to formal mathematics too late to make major new contributions.

Exposure by itself is not sufficient, however much it may seem to be the case for even the most talented individuals. In cases of the most remarkable early performance, continuous, careful instructional assistance is the rule. The instruction need not be formal in all instances. If books, aids, models, and so forth are available, a child may be self-taught in a sense that no teacher devising an individualized curriculum or regime of practice has ever equaled, but even in these rare instances the child benefits from a history of pedagogy in a field. As he moved toward becoming a grandmaster, for example, Bobby Fischer was able to study on his own hundreds of books and articles on chess technique, chess history, and current analyses of important games. (Fischer, by the way, was not entirely self-educated. He was taught for several years by more advanced masters who were also highly skilled teachers.) Instruction of some sort, then is necessary for progress through the advanced levels of specific, nonuniversal domains, even for gifted individuals with specific talent. Typically, individuals who perform at a very high level acknowledge the contributions of mentors who made their achievements possible; these contributions are quite literally true and not, as often believed, a matter of excessive modesty or self-effacement.

Finally, historical and cultural forces are critical to the recognition and development of talent. At some points in time, one field is stagnant while another is booming. These changes can be cyclical or not. There may never be another time, for example, when representational art holds the place that it did between the fifteenth and eighteenth centuries. Physics seemed to wane in our own midcentury disillusionment with nuclear warfare, yet surged again as laser technology, astrophysics, and basic issues about the nature of matter were reexplored. The timing of talent, tradition, and history is critical, as is the culture within which it grows. If Einstein had been raised as a Buddhist in Thailand, would he have mastered western physics? If Mozart had been a tribal chieftain in Africa, or for that matter a woman in Austria, would he have written great symphonies? If Gandhi has been reared on a farm in Kansas, would he have transformed a whole society? These examples may seem whimsical if not silly, but I mean them to be taken quite seriously. What we know about the biological evolution of ability would suggest that any of these events might have occurred (Washburn and Howell, 1960). My purpose is not to detract from the importance of individual talent in achievement or of genetics in contributing to talent but only to point out how precise the concentration of forces must be if remarkable achievements are to occur. Elsewhere I have referred to this process as *coincidence* (Feldman, 1979a, 1980a).

When giftedness or creativity of a high order occurs, it is because a number of forces such as those I have already mentioned have been brought into sustained, subtle, and delicate coordination. When the unique intellectual, emotional, social, and spiritual qualities of an individual are treated in just the right way by those who are crucial to the process, and when this occurs at a time and place when the qualities can be uniquely expressed through a given domain, then this *coincidence* may lead to remarkable achievement. More typically, of course, coordination and expression is less than optimal and less remarkable work is done. I have likened this process to the most delicate ballet imaginable. It might also be thought of as the sublimely intricate sequencing and coordination of messages transmitted by the genetic material in the nucleus of every cell.

The process of development in the Piagetian sense is incredibly robust (as it would have to be to claim universality); where the expression of extraordinary talent is concerned, the process is incredibly delicate. If any of the forces I have described (and no doubt others as well) is not in near perfect coordination with the others in its timing, sequencing, duration, intensity, and specificity, the chances are greatly reduced for full expression of talent and, as a consequence, for great achievements and creative contributions.

If it is true that little is known about the properties of nonuniversal developmental domains, it is also true that our knowledge of the interactions of those forces that stimulate development is miniscule. As an agenda for research on giftedness is established, somewhere near the top should be the study of the nature and quality of environmental forces as they interact with talent and personality to produce (or prevent) remarkable achievement.

## Stages

Some researchers have sought to join Piagetian and psychometric views by looking for indications that gifted (high IQ) children move through Piagetian stages more quickly than others. The evidence for this assumption is weak, however, and for the most part negative (Gottfried and Brody, 1975). High IQ and average IQ children of the same age typically score at the same stage on Piagetian measures (see Keating, 1975; Kohlberg and De Vries, 1971).

However, if we dismiss the notion of gifted children as high IQ children and we modify the Piagetian notion of stage, some interesting patterns begin to emerge. Again, evidence from children who are undisputedly gifted—prodigies—provides little support for the existence of acceleration on broad Piagetian tests of reasoning. My subjects performed much like other bright children their age on both IQ tests and Piaget-based measures. In their specialties, however, these children had reached stages of mastery usually achieved only by highly competent adults in the field (Feldman, 1979a, 1980a). An eight-year-old chess player, for example, reasoned at the concrete operations stage on Piagetian measures, and his school records showed high but not extremely high IQ and achievement scores; yet in chess he was a B level player with 1300+ points and was rated higher than many adult opponents on the tournament circuit.

Prodigies are thus problematic for Piaget's theory. For example, Piaget assumes that the development of the broad, general structures must be completed before they can be applied to a specific domain such as chess, music, law, or physics (Piaget, 1972). Prodigies seem to contradict this assumption. They perform at a high level in their specific fields, but at an age-appropriate level on Piagetian stage measures. Furthermore, the fields in which the prodigies in my study perform (chess, music composition, natural science, prose writing) are among the more "resistant" to application of mental structures (Feldman, 1980a). That a child would perform at an adult level on a chess board but at a child's level on standard tests of role taking, map drawing, combinational ability, and moral judgment suggests that development can proceed rapidly in a specific field without bringing the whole of cognitive development along with it. Whatever processes account for movement to more advanced stages of chess playing, for example, these processes do not seem to have the same effect on the more general process of thinking that they do in this specific area of chess playing. As Gardner (see his chapter in the present volume), Turiel (1977), and I (Feldman, 1980a) have recently argued, it may be wise to consider various domains as having independent developmental trajectories. For the study of giftedness this would seem to make a great deal of sense.

Here, then, is another place where a modification of Piagetian theory seems to be necessary to accommodate the gifted. Piaget's concept of stage is intended to capture the sequence of universal changes in mental structure that occur as the child matures. Another way of thinking about stages is to conceptualize them as existing within specific fields or domains, thus allowing one to chart progress in a particular field without necessarily drawing implications about development in any others. To see stages in this way means abandoning one of Piaget's purposes — characterizing the universal sequence of stages in cognitive development — and focusing instead on less common, domain-specific changes (Feldman, 1980b).

By focusing on specific domains, we can study more circumscribed forms of talent without necessarily needing to invoke the existence of high general abilities. This arrangement seems to square better with the facts than traditional high IQ conceptions of giftedness; although many people who are highly accomplished in a specific field also have high IQ's, many do not. Child prodigies and savants sometimes represent extreme examples of this. Applying stage sequential analyses to specific domains is one approach to understanding better the course of change within a field without being inevitably tied to general conceptions of intelligence or cognitive development.

In fact, little is known about the possible stage sequential nature of specific fields or domains. Piaget set a high standard for developmental theory by insisting on a rich account of processes available to the child at each stage. It is not enough to say that a student is a neophyte physicist; one must describe the thinking processes about physics that are available to that student, distinguish these from later, more sophisticated stages, and embed them all within a theory of development of physics understanding so that the course of change is coherent and comprehensible. Comparable analyses for each domain of interest would be required to establish its sequence of stages. Presumably, some domains would have certain similar processes of thought, parallel sequences, and so forth, but this remains to be seen. (See also the chapter by Gardner in this volume.).

Thinking of stages as residing within domains portrays giftedness as assuming many guises. Every field has a special vocabulary for its levels and capabilities: One has an "ear" for music, a "nose" for problems in science, "chess sense," "intuition" in mathematics, "elegance" in computer programming and mathematics, "timing" in comedy and storytelling, and so forth. Perhaps a place to begin a domain-based study of stages is with these kinds of specialized terms—determining how they are used and their qualities are judged. If there is consensus by experts on the meanings of such terms (and I believe that within limits such consensus will be found), they can be used to help build a psychology of domains that encompasses the full range of talent.

Admittedly we have moved a long way from Piaget's stages, and this line of reasoning is of course highly speculative; much research is needed to assess the usefulness of stage notions for characterizing various fields of endeavor and the distinctiveness (or lack of it) of each domain. My purpose here is to suggest possibilities, however, and to sketch a developmental framework that might guide future research in giftedness and creativity. Since some concept of stage is so central to most developmental theories, it is difficult to imagine a framework that is developmental (in Piaget's sense) and at the same time stageless (Feldman, 1979a; Flavell, 1971; Kessen, 1962). A domain-specific orientation to cognitive development is one way to retain stages yet not ignore the uniqueness of every genuine domain (Feldman, 1980a).

## Transitions and Creativity

Piaget offered the process of equilibration as a mechanism for the development of thought processes of each stage. This process, as with other features of his theory, is governed by the intrinsic tendency of the individual to structure knowledge. Depending upon what structures are available and what the situation presents, the child will assimilate information to existing structures, or change structures, or in most cases do both to some extent. Only within the functional range of the child's existing structures can information be utilized in the equilibration process. Yet every child actually creates at least four quite distinct mental systems, not out of whole cloth necessarily but not out of anything given from the environment either. Indeed, Piaget was puzzled all his life by the appearance in development of what he called *novelties*—that is, qualitatively distinct mental functions that cannot be explained as either strictly maturational or environmental in origin but that somehow emerge from the child's efforts to comprehend the world (Piaget, 1971).

Novelties in the sense that Piaget wrote of them could also be called creations, as common as such maturational achievements as walking or smiling perhaps, but creations still. This form of creation is of course not what is usually meant by the term *creativity*, but within the expanded view of development proposed in this chapter there may be links between novelties or creations in the Piagetian sense and creative achievements in the more exalted sense that we typically use the term. Consider for a moment the fact that creativity is itself often meant in two senses: One refers to a protean vitality and expressiveness that is a general human quality; the other refers to a significant contribution to a significant body of knowledge and skill. A four-year-old's colorful, dramatic, and expressive drawing of animals in the zoo reflects creativity in the first sense. And it is this sense of creativity that romantic educational writers invoke when claiming that all children can learn, can become distinct and unique individuals, can make their own decisions about what to learn and when and how to learn it (see, for example, Feldman, 1979b). Michelangelo's "David" is an extraordinary example of creativity in the second sense.

Given the expanded view of development proposed in this chapter, it would make sense to consider creativity of both the mundane and the more lofty varieties as the product of developmental processes. In fact there are now three kinds of reorganizations to be considered, all of which seem related to creativity. First are the transitions between Piagetian stages that, however common, reflect the appearance of universally achieved novelties in thinking. Next are transitions between stages within nonuniversal developmental domains, the reorganizations in understanding that are achieved by those who strive to master these more optional bodies of knowledge. Finally — and I think most relevant for the field of giftedness and creativity — are those relatively rare occasions when one has mastered a domain through all its existing stages, but a state of disequilibrium persists because of an unsolved problem, puzzle, or conundrum. When one fashions a way to go beyond the current state of knowledge of the field, creativity in the third and most unusual sense is in evidence (Feldman, 1980a). An assumption of this chapter is that fundamentally similar transition processes are at work when all three kinds of creativity occur, and that understanding one kind should help in understanding the others (although see Gruber, 1980).

In its most powerful form creativity is the extension of a body of knowledge beyond the structural borders that preceded its appearance. Thus, creativity in the sense of major new contribution is built out of mastery of a field or domain — that is, is a further expression of giftedness rather than a totally separate process. It is one more transition in a lifetime of transitions, some mundane and some profound. If the expression of giftedness is reflected in mastery of advanced levels of challenging domains, then the fullest expression of giftedness is reflected in attempts to transform a domain and enhance its usefulness.

We may even suppose that the formulation of a powerful, new, qualitatively distinct reorganization of an entire significant domain might be a reasonable way to define genius. After Darwin, much of biological knowledge had to be reorganized; after Freud, our knowledge of human motivation was recast; after Einstein, knowledge of certain kinds of interactions in the physical world was reconceptualized. All creativity, then, represents a partial accommodation, an extension of a field, while genius represents a total reorganization. At least conceptually, this seems to place giftedness, creativity, and genius into a coherent relationship with one another.

Seen as expressions of fundamentally similar developmental processes, the three — giftedness, creativity, genius — express relative degrees of movement through domains. Roughly speaking, giftedness (if it is developed) refers to the achievement of advanced levels of mastery in a specified domain — for example, a successful concert pianist or chef in a major restaurant. Creativity goes beyond this level to include the addition of new meaning to the existing domain: a concert pianist's interpretation of a Mozart sonata that finds new, fresh meaning in the classical piece, or a chef who invents an entirely new style of preparation. Genius represents the transformation of an entire domain so that it must be reorganized altogether, and from that point forward the domain as transformed will be what is passed on to new learners. The invention of the keyboard, the creation of *haute cuisine* — these begin to reflect the qualities of genius that I wish to suggest. Clearer examples come from scientific efforts such as the theory of relativity, evolution by natural selection, unconscious motivation, and the double helix model of DNA, to mention some of the more prominent discoveries of the last 150 years.

Given the view of transitions and creativity proposed here, a number of questions become interesting for research: How similar are the conditions that set off reorganizations in one domain (say numerical understanding) to transitions in another (say chess)? What kinds of limitations, if any, operate against advancement in more specific domains when an individual has not achieved the most advanced Piagetian stage? To what extent are the transition processes similar for talented individuals and for less talented ones? How related are rapid movement through the Piagetian stages and the quality of later performance in a field? And are there characteristics of the occurrence of genius or conditions that catalyze it that might help us understand better how and when such major reorganizations might occur (Gruber, 1974)?

Piaget acknowledged that he was unable to show how novelties were possible and how they were formed. "For example," he wrote, "I must try to explain, starting the simple psychological function, how Cantor came to create the set theory" (1971, p. 194). Notice that the example Piaget chose to illustrate novelties in thought (and many of his other examples as well) comes from a nonuniversal domain. No conservation problem exists here, with its inevitable achievement and spontaneous appearance. Set theory is understood by few who are not taught it and chosen as an area of specialization by a tiny number of mathematicians. Piaget's theoretical stance required that nonuniversal achievements, including creative ones such as the invention of set theory, be analyzed as if they were universal achievements, based on the simple psychological function referred to in the quote. The view proposed in this chapter makes a different assumption — that similar processes of change account for both universal and nonuniversal achievements, but that the conditions that give rise to these changes, the structure of each of the domains, and the qualities of the individual working to achieve them, may have distinctive qualities that cannot be reduced to those of any other domain. I would argue that Piaget was never able to explain Cantor's discovery because he was searching in the wrong place. The simple psychological function has little to do specifically with advanced mathematical reasoning.

Instead, by studying directly the development of the successive structures of mathematical thinking acquired by students of mathematics, the process that led Cantor to create set theory may be more fully revealed. In addition, since transitions in reasoning about mathematics (and in every other nonuniversal domain) are not effected without powerful catalytic forces operating in the environment, catalytic conditions may be more fully available for analysis because of the contributions of these external forces. And what is true for mathematics should be true (although not identically so) for other domains. Knowledge about reorganization and transformation of bodies of knowledge through processes of construction and interaction should reveal a great deal about giftedness and creativity. Piaget seemed to sense that this step needed to be taken although he was unable to do so in his lifetime.

## Conclusion

It has been my purpose in this chapter to present a developmental point of view to guide inquiry into giftedness and creativity. Psychometric views, however useful they may have been in the past, are unlikely to lead to further understanding of extraordinary capability and exceptional achievement. Although at first glance Piaget's view of intellectual development seems remote from giftedness and creativity, I have tried to show that this is not altogether true. Proposing extensions of Piaget's notions of stage, interaction, and transition provides us with elements for building a developmental framework that encompasses the extremes in ability and performance as well as the common achievements, the unique and extraordinary uses of human capability as well as the common universal ones.

There is another feature of the developmental approach to giftedness that may be particularly important: The developmental framework described here (and no doubt others as well) is inherently humane in its assumptions. I have claimed elsewhere that genuine acceptance and appreciation of differences in ability and performance requires that the differences be non-threatening (Feldman, 1979b). If every person believed that he or she had unique potentials and that the expression of potential was achieved when a culture committed itself to assisting in the delicate coordination of evolution, individual propensity, history, tradition, culture, instruction, mentors, and institutions, then the likelihood of resentment and ambivalence toward excellence would be vastly reduced. A developmental view of giftedness and creativity offers one way of giving full credit to the unique personal qualities that lead individuals to do remarkable things, while also recognizing that the individual's ability to use his or her potential is a gift born of time and place that transcends even the most extraordinary of talents. Although this may seem a somewhat inspirational way to end what is a sober, analytic treatment of the topic of giftedness and creativity, inspiration too has a place when the task ahead is to rejuvenate a field of inquiry; and it is toward that end that this chapter and the other contributions to the present volume are aimed.

## References

Bandura, A. *Social Learning Theory*. Englewood Cliffs, N.J.: Prentice-Hall, 1977.

Bringuier, J. *Conversations with Jean Piaget*. Chicago: University of Chicago Press, 1980.

Case, R. "Intellectual Development from Birth to Adulthood: A Neo-Piagetian Interpretation." In R. S. Siegler (Ed.), *Children's Thinking: What Develops?* Hillsdale, N.J.: Erlbaum, 1978.

Cowan, P. *Piaget with Feeling*. New York: Holt, Rinehart and Winston, 1978.

Damon, W. "Patterns of Change in Children's Social Reasoning." *Child Development*, 1980, *51*, 1010–1017.

Feldman, D. H. "Faulty Construction: A Review of Wallach and Wing's *The Talented Student*." *Contemporary Psychology*, 1970, *15*, 3–4.

Feldman, D. H. "Universal to Unique: A Developmental View of Creativity and Education." In S. Rosner and L. Abt (Eds.), *Essays in Creativity*. Croton-on-Hudson, N.Y.: North River Press, 1974.

Feldman, D. H. "The Child as Craftsman." *Phi Delta Kappan*, 1976, *58*, 143–149.

Feldman, D. H. "Review of W. Dennis' and M. Dennis' *The Intellectually Gifted: An Overview*." *Harvard Educational Review*, 1977, *47*, 576–581.

Feldman, D. H. "The Mysterious Case of Extreme Giftedness." In H. Passow (Ed.), *The Gifted and the Talented: Yearbook of the National Society for the Study of Education*. Chicago: University of Chicago Press, 1979a.

Feldman, D. H. "Toward a Nonelitist Conception of Giftedness." *Phi Delta Kappan*, 1979b, *60*, 660–663.

Feldman, D. H. *Beyond Universals in Cognitive Development*. Norwood, N.J.: Ablex, 1980a.

Feldman, D. H. "Stage and Transition in Cognitive-Developmental Research: Getting to the Next Level." *Genetic Epistemologist*, 1980b, *9*, 1–6.

Feldman, D. H. "A Study of Subjects in the Terman Sample Who Scored Above 180 IQ." Unpublished manuscript.

Feldman, D. H., and Levin, D. "The Young Child as Craftsman: Extension of a Metaphor." Presented at the University of Maryland Conference of Research in Early Childhood Education, College Park, April 1977.

Fischer, K. W. "A Theory of Cognitive Development: The Control and Construction of Hierarchies of Skills." *Psychological Review*, 1980, *87*, 477–531.

Fischer, K. W. (Ed.). *New Directions for Child Development: Cognitive Development*, no. 12. San Francisco: Jossey-Bass, 1981.

Flavell, J. *The Developmental Psychology of Jean Piaget*. New York: D. Van Nostrand, 1963.

Flavell, J. "Stage-Related Properties of Cognitive Development." *Cognitive Psychology*, 1971, *2*, 421–453.

Gardner, H. *The Quest for Mind*. New York: Vintage, 1972.

Gardner, H. "Prodigies' Progress." *Psychology Today*, May 1981, 75–79.

Gardner, H., Wolf, D., and Smith, N. "Artistic Symbols in Early Childhood." *New York University Education Quarterly*, 1975, *6*, 13–21.

Gottfried, A. W., and Brody, N. "Interrelationships Between Correlates of Psychometric and Piagetian Scales of Sensorimotor Intelligence." *Developmental Psychology,* 1975, *11,* 379–387.

Gruber, H. E. "Afterword." In D. H. Feldman, *Beyond Universals in Cognitive Development.* Norwood, N.J.: Ablex, 1980.

Gruber, H. E. *Darwin on Man: A Psychological Study of Scientific Creativity.* (2nd ed.) Chicago: University of Chicago Press, 1981.

Guilford, J. P. "Creativity." *American Psychologist,* 1950, *5,* 444–454.

Jensen, A. R. "How Much Can We Boost IQ and Scholastic Achievement?" *Harvard Educational Review,* 1969, *39,* 1–123.

Keating, D. "Precocious Cognitive Development at the Level of Formal Operations." *Child Development,* 1975, *46,* 276–280.

Kessen, W. "*Stage* and *Structure* in the Study of Children." In W. Kessen and C. Kuhlman (Eds.), *Thought in the Young Child. Monographs of the Society for Research in Child Development,* 1962, *27,* 53–70.

Kohlberg, L. and DeVries, R. "Relations Between Piaget and Psychometric Assessments of Intelligence." In C. Lavatelli (Ed.), *The Natural Curriculum.* Urbana, Ill.: ERIC Center for Early Childhood Education, 1971.

Kohlberg, L., and Mayer, R. "Development as the Aim of Education." *Harvard Educational Review,* 1972, *42,* 449–496.

Langer, J. "Disequilibrium as a Source of Development." In P. Mussen, J. Langer, and M. Covington (Eds.), *Trends and Issues in Developmental Psychology.* New York: Holt, Rinehart and Winston, 1969.

Moessinger, P. "Piaget on Equilibration." *Human Development,* 1978, *21,* 255–267.

Piaget, J. "The Theory of Stages in Cognitive Development." In D. Green, M. Ford, and G. Flamer (Eds.), *Measurement and Piaget.* New York: McGraw-Hill, 1971.

Piaget, J. "Intellectual Evolution from Adolescence to Adulthood." *Human Development,* 1972, *15,* 1–12.

Piaget, J. *The Development of Thought: Equilibration of Cognitive Structures.* New York: Viking, 1975.

Renzulli, J. S. "Will the Gifted Child Movement Be Alive and Well in 1980?" *Gifted Child Quarterly,* 1980, *21,* 3–9.

Scarr, S., and Weinberg, R. A. "IQ Test Performance of Black Children Adopted by White Families." *American Psychologist,* 1976, *31,* 726–739.

Sears, P. S. "The Terman Genetic Studies of Genius, 1922–1972." In H. Passow (Ed.), *The Gifted and the Talented.* Chicago: University of Chicago Press, 1979.

Siegler, R. "Developmental Sequences Within and Between Concepts." *Monographs of the Society for Research in Child Development,* 1981, *96* (2). Entire issue.)

Strauss, S. "Inducing Cognitive Development and Learning. I: The Organismic Developmental Approach." *Cognition,* 1972, *4,* 329–357.

Terman, L. M. "The Discovery and Encouragement of Exceptional Talent." *American Psychologist,* 1954, *9,* 221–230.

Turiel, E. "Developmental Processes in the Child's Moral Thinking." In P. Mussen, J. Langer, and M. Covington (Eds.), *Trends and Issues in Developmental Psychology.* New York: Holt, Rinehart and Winston, 1969.

Turiel, E. "Conflict and Transition in Adolescent Moral Development." *Child Development,* 1974, *45,* 14–29.

Turiel, E. "Distinct Conceptual and Developmental Domains: Social Convention and Morality." In C. B. Keasey (Ed.), *Nebraska Symposium on Motivation.* Lincoln: University of Nebraska Press, 1977.

Vygotsky, L. S. *Thought and Language.* Cambridge, Mass.: M.I.T. Press, 1962. (First published in 1932.)

Wallach, M. A. *The Creativity-Intelligence Distinction.* New York: General Learning Press, 1971.

Washburn, S., and Howell, F. "Human Evolution and Culture." In S. Tax (Ed.), *The Evolution of Man.* Vol. 2. Chicago: University of Chicago Press, 1960.

Witty, P. "Contributions to the IQ Controversy from the Study of Superior Deviates." *School and Society,* 1940, *51,* 503–508.

*David Henry Feldman is associate professor,*
*Eliot-Pearson Department of Child Study,*
*Tufts University.*

*Recent neurobiological findings permit speculation on the existence*
*of several distinct realms of competence, each developing at its*
*own pace and in its own way. Combined with a spirit of*
*playfulness, giftedness may develop from any*
*combination of these sources.*

# Giftedness: Speculations
# from a Biological Perspective

*Howard Gardner*

Imagine a musical audition where the judges are barred from viewing the con-
testants. In this case, the candidates happen to be kindergartners. The first one
plays the violin, the second plays a piano composition of his own, the third sings
an aria with exquisite pitch, rhythm, and verbal articulation. Though clearly
different, the achievements of these three children sound equally impressive to
the "blind" judges.

Once additional information has been provided, however, the significance of each of these youthful performances takes on a different flavor. Suppose
that the first performer is a young Japanese child who has been enrolled since
the age of two in an intensive Suzuki Talent Education program. Suppose that
the second child is a precocious composer, reminiscent of the youthful Mozart or
Mendelssohn. And suppose that the third child is a victim of infantile autism, a
child incapable of normal communication or problem solving, but able to repro-
duce entire compositions perfectly upon a single hearing. Thus we have three

Preparation of this chapter was supported by a grant from the Bernard van
Leer Foundation of the Hague to the Harvard Graduate School of Education. Research
described was supported by grants from the Spencer Foundation, the Carnegie Corporation, the National Institute of Education, the National Institute of Neurological Diseases, Communication Disorders, and Stroke, and the Veterans Administration.

D. Feldman (Ed.). *New Directions for Child Development: Developmental Approaches to Giftedness and Creativity,* no. 17.
San Francisco: Jossey-Bass, September 1982.

**47**

impressive music achievements, presumably achieved by three disparate musical routes in a trio of children.

Speculating, we may say that, in the case of the autistic child, we behold the expression or amplification of a single inborn gift with relatively little influence from the child's particular environment or training (Park, 1978; Rimland, 1964). In the case of the Suzuki child, we encounter a virtually opposite set of circumstances: A child of average proclivities has been subjected to an extremely intensive training regimen that produces performances of very high quality (Suzuki, 1964; Taniuchi, 1981). Finally, in the case of a child prodigy such as Mozart, there seems to be a happy cooccurrence, or "coincidence" (Feldman, 1980), of several factors: inborn proclivities, intensive efforts, suitable models, and an environment replete with supportive parents, siblings, patrons, and other individuals in the culture. To reduce this to a simple-minded formula, the Suzuki child is a triumph of his or her environment, the autistic child is a product of biology, the child prodigy, a happy combination of multiple factors.

Though the case can be made dramatically with music, a similar trio of individuals could be assembled in other domains of competence. For example, in the area of the visual arts, one can cite an autistic child such as the gifted artist Nadia (Selfe, 1977); a child growing up in an intensive artistic atmosphere such as Bali (Belo, 1937; Gardner, 1980; McPhee, 1938); or a young prodigy such as Picasso or Klee (Gardner, 1980). In fact, even outside the arts, in domains such as mathematics, chess, or expository writing, one may find a comparable range of gifts and sources.

But, the reader may properly protest, if there is any area in science in which we have transcended simple dichotomies, it is in the area of human achievements. Any attempt to tease out heredity from environment to apportion the responsibility to one or the other, is futile. All development involves interaction: Genetics could not exist without expression in an environment; environmental effects could not exist except with reference to a genetic program. Contemplating the very same example, moreover, one could draw radically different implications about sources. Thus, in the case of Mozart, from one point of view the potential inheres in the child's genome: Surely, not every Salzburg youth could have composed full-length operas when barely pubescent. Yet, if we simply shift the perspective a bit, we can see that the potential exists as well in the environment, parental household, and the culture. The genetic Mozart, in Pharaonic Egypt, might not have composed at all. Why resurrect an outmoded distinction?

The intent here is rather different. I seek not to ascertain or demonstrate the genetics of giftedness, but rather to determine the extent to which one may profitably consider gifts or talents from a biological perspective, to assess the biological contributions to unusual, even prodigious achievement. From the perspective of mainstream developmental psychology, this will involve two reorientations—first, a willingness to pay more than lip service to factors of biology, including genetics and neurobiology; second, an inclination to consider cognitive achievements of a diverse sort, at many levels of competence.

## Biology: The View from Genetics

Any biological treatment must proceed from the child's genetic proclivity for elaborating certain kinds of competences. Yet the evidence currently available from genetics does not furnish sufficient information about the attainment and expression of gifts (Brooks, 1980). Of course, genetics affects every aspect of life including the existence, attainment, and versatility of skills, be they those of the artist, the physicist, or the athlete. With humans, however, it is not possible to carry out experiments that allow us to ascertain the extent to which a particular trait is heritable within a population (Block and Dworkin, 1976; Gould, 1981; Lewontin, 1970). Even though there have been speculations about the extent to which, for example, musical giftedness is a hereditary ability (Gerard, 1952), these are likely to remain untested.

Genetics has proved most successful at studying simple traits, the kinds that are borne by a specific gene or specific loci on a chromosome. Even in animals, more complex traits, skills, or patterns of behavior have resisted genetic analysis. The kinds of gifts of concern here are polymorphous traits that are undoubtedly carried by many genes or combinations of genes and can only be expressed as a result of highly complex interactions with an environment. Even the striking findings recently obtained from the study of identical and fraternal twins have made but a modest contribution to our understanding of the origins of highly developed cognitive skills (Chen, 1979; Scarr-Salapatek, 1975).

Nonetheless, a genetic perspective may provide a useful metaphor for an inquiry about giftedness. It is well known that, as a result of heredity, certain individuals are at risk for certain diseases. This does not mean that the individual will necessarily acquire the disease: Rather, it suggests that, given two individuals raised in the same environment, the individual at risk stands a much higher likelihood of contracting the disease than the individual with a contrasting genetic background. Moreover, the chances of the disease spreading rapidly and being fatal also differ markedly across individuals drawn from different populations (Gajdusek, 1968).

In line with some current speculations (Fowler, 1981), I propose that certain individuals be viewed as "at promise" for the attainment of exceedingly high levels of skill. An individual "at promise" will not necessarily become an accomplished chess player, musician, mathematician, or painter. Despite his or her increased susceptibility, he or she must still be exposed to the relevant materials and have an opportunity to explore them. However, with minimal exposure, individuals "at promise" should advance very rapidly in various domains. They may well also display an insistent, single-minded sense of purpose that readily distinguishes them from other individuals, who, when exposed to the same materials, will make much less rapid and focalized advances. Still, even here, the environment matters. Two individuals "at promise" for success in chess are likely to achieve different rates of growth, depending upon whether they happen to be reared in a major metropolitan area with a sizable Russian Jewish population or a rural region in a preliterate culture.

## A Neurobiological Perspective

While genetics proves a logical point of departure for a biological inquiry into giftedness, it is in fact the areas of neurobiology — neuroanatomy, neurophysiology, and neuropsychology — that at present hold greater promise for an elucidation of giftedness. These are areas in which considerable progress has recently been made in the understanding of both human and infrahuman abilities and in which the gap between gene and gift is not nearly as pronounced. (For a useful survey, see *Scientific American,* September 1980). From my point of view, the work in neurobiology signals the need for rethinking certain assumptions within the area of psychology.

## The Notion of Separate Domains

In many areas of psychology, there has been a long-standing tendency to think of all forms of knowledge as comparable to one another and, correlatively, to treat all portions of the nervous system as equally suited for the acquisition and transmission of diverse forms of knowledge. These points of view go back many decades and pervade much psychological and psychobiological writing (Head, 1963; Lenneberg, 1967).

The tendency I have just described takes two forms. On the one hand, there is the view stated most baldly by behaviorists such as B. F. Skinner (1953) that the constitution of the nervous system — the "black box" — is of no interest to psychologists and that events in the brain are essentially irrelevant to an understanding of human behavior (and thought). Within the area of neuropsychology, there is a related perspective, strongly propounded by Lashley (1929): The brain is an equipotential organ, such that virtually any human ability can be subserved by any portion of the brain. According to this view, recently revived by the psychologist of language, Lenneberg (1967), the notion of neural plasticity, particularly among the young, has been unduly emphasized. Consequently, researchers have ignored or minimized the possibility that different zones of the brain might subserve specific and different capacities.

Within the study of cognition, there has been an equally strong and pervasive tendency to lump together all manner of human intellectual abilities. The intelligence testing (or IQ tradition) harbors long-standing belief in a general ($g$) factor of intelligence along which people can be arrayed (Spearman, 1904). True, many researchers also believe in the existence of more specific factors (Thurstone and Thurstone, 1941), but even these researchers subscribe to the notion that there exist general psychological processes such as perception, memory, learning, and so forth that cut across the specific factors.

In a curious way, the Piagetian perspective has also contributed to this widespread consensus about the unitary quality of cognition. Piaget (1970) believed in extremely general mental operations that cut across all the domains of knowledge of interest to him — for example, number, causality, moral judgments, social understanding, and the like. There is no notion here of individual abilities developing at their own rate in disparate domains. Instead, one encounters a belief in a single central processor that unfolds according to a preordained program and is manifest in all mental activities of importance to human beings.

I do not wish to deny the important contributions made by Lashley, Piaget, and the intelligence testing movement. Nonetheless, in my view, the pervasiveness of their approach has blinded observers to an opposing set of truths, the existence of relatively independent domains of knowledge. (For a similar view, see Allport, 1980; Fodor, 1981.) The case for these domains needs to be made if a better understanding of the nature and development of giftedness is to be forthcoming.

## Domains as Spheres of Competence

I propose that human cognitive competence be thought of as consisting of a number of autonomous, or semiautonomous, domains of intellect. Each of these intellectual competences has its own genetic origins and limitations as well as its own neuroanatomical substrate or substrates. At the psychological level of analysis, each domain entails its own specific symbol system (or systems), which the individual must master; and, at the societal level of study, each domain can be drawn on in order to achieve the particular competences valued in each human culture.

These intellectual competences or "intelligences" have evolved over millions of years in order to carry out specific hominoid problem-solving and production activities, including finding one's way around an environment, making tools, and communicating and interacting successfully with other individuals. They have precursors in other species, but in each case they have developed along specific lines within the human species. All normal individuals possess some potential for developing each of the intellectual competences, but individuals differ from one another in the extent to which they can and will realize each competence, even as their cultures and subcultures differ in the extent to which they value disparate intellectual competences and sets of competences.

For present purposes, the precise identity and identification of these particular intellectual competences is less crucial than an acknowledgement of the existence, importance, and semiautonomy of some such family of "intelligences." The case for their identity will be made elsewhere (Gardner, in preparation *a* and *b*). But simply to give an indication of the kind of intellectual skill I have in mind — the level of generality at which I am speaking and the sort of individual who exemplifies a particular competence — let me nominate seven candidates for autonomous human intellectual competences:

1. Linguistic competence, such as that exhibited by writers and public speakers;

2. Musical competence, such as that found in composers and performers;

3. Mathematical-logical competence, or the kinds of problem-solving abilities studied by Piaget and realized to a high degree by scientists;

4. Visual-spatial competence, such as the ability to envision and transform visual-spatial representations found in architects and engineers;

5. Bodily-kinesthetic competence, such as the abilities exploited by athletes and dancers;

6. Social-interpersonal competence, or the abilities needed for successful interaction with other individuals, such as the skills found in politicians;

7. Intrapersonal competence, or knowledge of and access to one's own feelings and desires; self-knowledge.

The way in which one conceptualizes these candidate competences will differ, depending upon the scientific perspective that is assumed. From a biological perspective, these competences may be thought of as raw computational abilities, information-processing devices that operate (almost reflexively) upon information obtained from the environment and also from the organism. The syntactic processes studied by psychologists (Fodor, Bever, and Garrett, 1974) and the visual transformations studied by experimental psychologists (Kosslyn, 1980; Shepard and Metzler, 1971) provide insight into the kinds of processes that may be subserved by these computational mechanisms. From the cultural perspective, these intelligences can be thought of as valued spheres of excellence or competence that every individual must acquire to some extent if he or she is to be able to negotiate his or her way successfully within the culture and that selected individuals are expected to master (Gladwin, 1970; Lave, 1977; Lord, 1960). In between the biological and the cultural, one finds a psychological perspective, that of symbol systems. The intelligences are embodied in the particular meaning, or symbolic systems, that a culture has devised over long periods of time and that individuals master by exercising their computational devices, singly and jointly (Gardner, 1979; Gardner, Howard, and Perkins, 1974).

This treatment in terms of different perspectives may be clarified by an example. Thus, the linguistic competence may be thought of biologically as drawing upon certain regions in the left hemisphere of the brain in order to carry out phonological and syntactic operations (Geschwind, 1970). Switching to a psychological (or symbol system) perspective, one treats linguistic competence as entailing the ability to speak, understand, and, eventually, read and write, and the capacity to produce speeches, stories, or sonnets. Finally, from the perspective of the overall culture, the linguistic abilities valued may include those of the poet, the public speaker, the political leader, or the inventor of new crossword puzzles.

No individual possesses equal potential in each of these domains. Individual profiles will vary markedly. Yet because all individuals have the capacity to attain some competence in each domain, information about the specific nature and operation of the intellectual competences is more likely to come from special populations — those in which particular competences have either been spared or destroyed in isolation. Indeed, the evidence for the present theory has come primarily from individuals with unusual gifts and disabilities: prodigies, highly gifted individuals, *idiot savants,* freaks and, above all, individuals with focal brain damage, which either spares or destroys in isolation one or more specific intellectual competences (Gardner, 1975). It is primarily from the examination of such populations that one can accrue evidence for the nature and the functioning of particular intellectual competences. In fact, in normal individuals, the devices work so well together and with such synchrony that their very existence tends to be obscured.

But while my belief in specific intellectual domains comes principally from neuropsychological studies with specific individuals, it should be stressed that this point of view draws on what may be an emerging consensus from a wider set of disciplines. From the point of view of neurology, there is increasing acceptance of the notion of specific neural regions that are anatomically, physiologically, and functionally distinct (Geschwind, 1965; Luria, 1966; Mountcastle, 1979). From the perspective of linguistics and philosophy, there is much discussion of the notion that intellectual domains can exist independently of one another, with each functioning according to its own rules and with little generalization of key components across these domains (Chomsky, 1980; Fodor, 1981; Sperber, 1974). Within psychology, an argument can be made that, rather than cutting across all domains, there are "vertical" forms of perception, learning, and memory that are specific to particular intellectual spheres (Fodor, 1981; Gardner, 1975). And certainly, within the anthropological perspective, there is considerable sympathy with the view that individuals can cultivate a wide range of cognitive skills with the particular choice constrained primarily by what is valued within a given culture (Cole and Means, 1981).

## The Development of Computational Devices:
## The Unfolding of Pure Gifts

In my view, there is a normal developmental course prescribed within each of these intellectual domains, each of these raw competences. The developmental course is determined along broad lines by genetic and neurobiological factors but presupposes the existence of an environment in which the particular intellectual competence can be cultivated. Consistent with the analyses of Piaget (1970) and Feldman (1980), I suggest that each domain can be viewed in terms of a stage sequence, with the earlier stages of competence available to all human beings simply by virtue of their growth in a human environment and with the later stages requiring more concentrated effort and, in many cases, specific tutelage. The degree of play or flexibility in the developmental trajectory within each domain may well vary substantially, depending, for example, on the nature and extent of early experience (Dennis, 1980; Changeux and Danchin, 1976; Goldman, 1979; Greenough and Juraska, 1979). Thus, healthy dosages of stimulation early in life have a very different effect from impoverishment in infancy or dosages available only in small amounts or only at later points in development (Denenberg, 1979; Rosenzweig, 1966). Moreover, domains may differ substantially from one another in the extent to which there is "play" for alternative routes of development. In the case of some domains, the lines of development are strictly laid down or, in biological terms, highly canalized (Waddington, 1962). In other domains, there may be considerable flexibility, and the end states that can be achieved are quite diverse.

Developmental progressions may reflect an interaction between factors of timing and plasticity. In the case of language, for example, an individual deprived of oral-aural stimulation may nonetheless develop a gestural system that bears significant parallels to ordinary syntax and semantics (Goldin-Meadow, Seligman, and Gelman, 1976). Here, clearly, is a testimonial to the power of canalization, for analogous principles have emerged despite the forced use of different physical systems for realization. But in the case of language, there is also neural plasticity early in life. Deprived of a left hemisphere, an individual will develop significant linguistic competence in his or her right hemisphere (Dennis, 1980; Woods and Teuber, 1978). However, if the left hemisphere is injured after the first several years of life, much less plasticity is exhibited and the individual will remain significantly aphasic. While other systems have not been carefully studied, one may anticipate similar tradeoffs between age and plasticity in other mental domains.

Even if, for analytic purposes, we describe each of these domains as developing along its own pristine path, it should be evident that, in normal development, there is considerable and increasing interaction among each of these domains. Indeed, nearly all human competences valued by cultures involve combinations of these intellectual devices. Almost never is a humanly valued skill dependent solely on one intellectual competence. (This is why *idiot savants* are so rarely capable of adequate functioning within a culture.) Thus, in considering the competences required by a lawyer, one can point to a number of crucial domains, including the linguistic, logical, and interpersonal realms. Lawyers will differ among one another substantially in the extent to which they rely on and exploit these particular intelligences. By the same token, the same intelligence may be harnessed to very different ends across individuals. The visual-spatial intelligence may be exploited in one way by an engineer, in a second way by a painter, and in yet other ways by an architect, a surgeon, or a weaver. In cultures with less division of labor, the interchangeability of intelligences may be even greater.

## Cultivating the Gift

The story of the growth and use of gifts is the story of how intelligences become socialized with a given human context. Cultures do not know of, or deal with, raw intelligences. They are concerned with roles and functions that must be carried out; these are identified by elders and presented to the young as end states towards which education and transmission of knowledge must be dedicated. What is instructive, from the point of view of a study of giftedness, are the ways in which these abilities are cultivated in individuals throughout the population: the special factors and maneuvers at work when an individual seems at promise for a certain gift (such as Mozart) and/or when a culture decides to invest a particular amount of energy or attention into a particular individual or a group of individuals (such as the Suzuki children).

According to this view of giftedness, an agenda follows for educational psychology. Investigators should focus on such issues as the early identification of individuals "at promise" within a domain; the devising of tests for their discovery; the laying out of specific training regimens; the devising of measures for assessing progress through a domain; and the analysis of the domain, such that particular deficits can be attacked, obviated, or compensated for.

Only part of the education of the gifted individual can be concerned with relatively pure computational considerations. While early development may reflect the operation of computational devices in a relatively untrammeled way, more general aspects of development will ultimately assume at least as much importance in the growth process. High motivation can compensate for inherently less powerful computation capacities; even as its absence will eventually frustrate even that individual who is most highly "at promise." The associated virtues of intention, purpose, will, and integrity become equally pivotal with the passage of time. The personality of the individual is also germane, particularly once the individual transcends the canonical steps within a given domain. For, ultimately, it is the individual's particular personal perspective upon events and attitude toward his or her chosen domain that will determine how finely articulated and original his or her contributions are. Naturally, cultures will differ from one another in the extent to which they value originality and imaginativeness as the end state of a domain or, alternatively, highlight the quintessential realization of an entrenched tradition. How these diverse states of development map onto the notion of a biologically driven computational device is a fascinating but as yet uninvestigated issue.

## Beyond the Framework: Future Studies

I have proposed here a novel and ambitious framework for the study of human gifts. In opposition to the notions that there exist extremely general human cognitive abilities and that an individual may be generally gifted or nongifted, I have posited the existence of semiautonomous domains of expertise rooted in biology. I have further claimed that individuals may be arrayed in terms of potential and ultimate achievement in each of them. The particular way in which these domains are codified and realized may differ radically across cultures, but there should exist ordered sequences of stages within domains, through which individuals must pass if they are to attain high levels of competence and become able to produce products of significance. Certain educational implications also follow from this framework, and these have been briefly sketched in this chapter.

Whatever its surface plausibility, however, this framework clearly stands in need of testing. In my own view, the most valuable insights concerning the framework are likely to emerge from case studies of individuals who stand out because of their gifts—individuals with distinctive profiles of gifts and individuals in diverse cultural settings. It is essential to discover the nature and functioning of these particular intellectual competences and to determine whether in fact they exhibit the kind of integrity, directedness, and sequence I have indicated. The only way in which this information can be gleaned is through intensive study of individuals who appear to possess instructive profiles of intellectual competence.

Important supporting information can, however, come from other sources. In nonhuman species, there are clear analogs to gifts. There are certain skills that are attained at high levels of competence by every individual within a species—for example, nut burying in squirrels. There are abilities at which every organism attains some skill but in which there are wide individual differences—for example, birdsong. And there are skills of a more "cultural" nature that only certain organisms within the species acquire the ability to carry out—for example, termite fishing in certain orders of chimpanzee. In these infrahuman organisms, it may prove possible to carry out genetic and neurobiological studies that would help fix the nature of the particular competences in question and might at the same time provide a biologically grounded way of thinking about the nature of talents and competences.

A second source of information concerning these intellectual competences would be studies of individuals who have the misfortune of being cognitively impaired due to inheritance, birth defects, or neural damage acquired later in life. By examining what these individuals can and cannot do and the routes they exploit in order to accomplish performances, researchers may secure valuable information about the nature of intellectual competences in gifted individuals.

A third area of insight could be obtained through work with normal individuals in an educational setting. Here, researchers could investigate what kinds of interventions, prosthetics, and alternative routes could be devised to help individuals ascend more rapidly within a given domain or compensate for an apparent lack of potential within a domain. Since there is flexibility for growth in any domain and since human beings are particularly flexible organisms, it would be important to determine the various ways in which a gift might be expressed, particularly in those individuals who are highly motivated for success (like our Suzuki child) but may not be "at promise" for success in that domain.

Returning for a moment, then, to our hypothetical audition, we may think of the young autistic child (be he a singer or she an artist) as an individual in whom a sheer "raw" intellectual competence has unfolded at great speed with relatively little input from the environment. The limits attained reflect our biological heritage, remote from environmental variations. In the case of the other two individuals, the environmental inputs are much more pronounced. In the case of Mozart, for example, one assumes that the environment and the neural computational mechanisms are working in consort. In the case of the Suzuki child, one may assume that the environment is providing the principal prosthetics and the push for maximum achievement that may not have been prefigured in (though it is of course allowed by) the individual's own genetic inheritance.

But there is one gift that all three of these individuals share—an important gift that should not be ignored in our neurobiological perspective. This is the gift of childhood—the proclivity, given to every human organism, to engage in free and spontaneous experimentation with physical and symbolic elements, the willingness to try out new arrangements, the absence of that hypercritical spirit that may dampen efforts at exploration, a ready access to one's emotional and affective experiences, and the eagerness to exploit culturally available means for expressing this feeling life. All of these are a special province of the young child and, regrettably, they are all too often lost as the years pass by. The gifted adult is that individual who retains much of the spirit and flexibility of the young child but has wedded it to high levels of achievement within a particular domain or set of domains. While the progress within the domain may to some extent be limited by the individual's genetic inheritance, the play and flexibility of early life is a gift that can be retained by every individual.

## References

Allport, D. A. "Patterns and Actions: Cognitive Mechanisms Are Content Specific." In G. Claxton (Ed.), *Cognitive Psychology: New Directions*. London: Routledge & Kegan Paul, 1980.

Belo, J. "Balinese Children's Drawing." *Djawa,* 1937, Nos. 5–6. (Entire issues.)

Block, N. J., and Dworkin, G. (Eds.). *The IQ Controversy.* New York: Pantheon, 1976.

Brooks, L. D. "Genetics and Human Populations." Unpublished manuscript, van Leer Project on Human Potential, Harvard Graduate School of Education, Harvard University, 1980.

Changeux, J. P., and Danchin, A. "Selective Stabilisation of Developing Synapses as a Mechanism for the Specification of Neuronal Networks." *Nature,* 1976, *264,* 705–712.

Chen, E. "Twins Reared Apart: A Living Lab." *New York Times Magazine,* December 9, 1979, 110–116.

Chomsky, N. *Rules and Representations.* New York: Columbia University Press, 1980.

Cole, M., and Means, B. *Comparative Studies of How People Think.* Cambridge: Harvard University Press, 1980.

Denenberg, V. "Animal Studies of Early Experience: Some Principles Which Have Implications for Human Development." In J. P. Hill (Ed.), *Minnesota Symposium on Child Psychology.* Vol. 3. Minneapolis: University of Minnesota Press, 1969.

Dennis, M. "Language Acquisition in the Single Hemisphere: Semantic Organization." In D. Caplan (Ed.), *Biological Studies of Mental Process.* Cambridge: M.I.T. Press, 1980.

Feldman, D. H. *Beyond Universals in Cognitive Development.* Norwood, N.J.: Ablex, 1980.

Fodor, J. "The Modularity of Mind." Unpublished manuscript, Massachusetts Institute of Technology, 1981.

Fodor, J., Bever, T., and Garrett, M. *The Psychology of Language.* New York: McGraw-Hill, 1974.

Fowler, W. "Early Identification and Stimulation of Talent in Children from Lower Education Black and White Families." Paper presented to the van Leer Project on Human Potential, Harvard Graduate School of Education, February 20, 1981.

Gajdusek, D. C. "Environmental Modification of Human Form and Function: The Problem of Coding in the Study of Patterning in Infancy of Nervous System Function." Paper presented at the First Plenary Session on Growth and Development, 12th International Congress of Pediatrics, Mexico, December 1968.

Gardner, H. *The Shattered Mind.* New York: Knopf, 1975.

Gardner, H. "Developmental Psychology After Piaget: An Approach in Terms of Symbolization." *Human Development,* 1979, *22,* 73–88.

Gardner, H. *Artful Scribbles: The Significance of Children's Drawings.* New York: Basic Books, 1980.

Gardner, H. "The Development of Competence in Culturally Defined Domains." In R. Shweder and R. LeVine (Eds.), *The Acquisition of Culture.* In preparation, *a.*

Gardner, H. "The Idea of Multiple Intelligences." Book manuscript, in preparation, *b.*

Gardner, H., Howard, V., and Perkins, D. "Symbol Systems: A Philosophical, Psychological, and Educational Investigation." In D. Olson (Ed.), *Media and Symbols: The Forms of Expression, Communication, and Education.* Chicago: University of Chicago Press, 1974.

Gerard, R. "The Biological Basis of Imagination." In B. Ghiselin (Ed.), *The Creative Process.* New York: Mentor, 1952.

Geschwind, N. "Disconnexion Syndromes in Animals and Man." *Brain,* 1965, *88,* 273–348; 585–644.

Geschwind, N. "The Organization of Language and the Brain." *Science,* 1970, *170,* 940–944.

Gladwin, T. *The East Is a Big Bird.* Cambridge: Harvard University Press, 1970.

Goldin-Meadow, S., Seligman, M.E.P., and Gelman, R. "Language in the Two-Year-Old." *Cognition,* 1976, *4,* 189–202.

Goldman, P. S. "Development and Plasticity of Frontal Association Cortex in the Infra-human Primate." In *The Neurological Bases of Language Disorders in Children.* Washington, D. C.: U.S. Department of Health, Education, and Welfare, NINCDS Monograph no. 22, 1979.

Gould, S. J. *The Mismeasure of Man.* New York: Norton, 1981.

Greenough, W. T., and Juraska, J. M. "Experience-Induced Changes in Brain Fine Structure: Their Behavioral Implications." In M. E. Hahn, C. Jensen, and B. C. Dudek (Eds.), *Development and Evolution of Brain Size: Behavioral Implications.* New York: Academic Press, 1979.

Head, H. *Aphasia and Kindred Disorders of Speech.* New York: Hafner, 1963. (Originally published 1926.)

Kosslyn, S. M. *Image and Mind.* Cambridge: Harvard University Press, 1980.

Lashley, K. *Brain Mechanisms and Intelligence.* Chicago: University of Chicago Press, 1929.

Lave, J. "Tailor-Made Experiments and Evaluating the Intellectual Consequences of Apprenticeship Training." *Quarterly Newsletter of the Institute for Comparative Human Development,* 1977, *1*, 1–3.

Lenneberg, E. *Biological Foundations of Language.* New York: Wiley, 1967.

Lewontin, R. "Race and Intelligence." *Bulletin of the Atomic Scientists,* March 1970, 2–8.

Lord, A. B. *The Singer of Tales.* Cambridge: Harvard University Press, 1960.

Luria, A. R. *The Higher Cortical Functions in Man.* New York: Basic Books, 1966.

McPhee, C. "Children and Music in Bali." *Djawa,* 1938, *18,* (6). (Entire issue.)

Mountcastle, V. B. "An Organizing Principle for Cerebral Function: The Unite Module and the Distributed System." In F. O. Schmitt (Ed.), *Neuroscience, Fourth Study Program.* Cambridge: M.I.T. Press, 1979.

Park, C. "Review of Nadia." *Journal of Autism and Childhood Schizophrenia,* 1978, *8,* 457–472.

Piaget, J. "Piaget's Theory." In P. Mussen (Ed.), *Carmichael's Manual of Child Psychology,* Vol. 1. New York: Wiley, 1970.

Rimland, B. *Infantile Autism.* New York: Appleton-Century-Crofts, 1964.

Rosenzweig, M. "Environmental Complexity, Cerebral Change, and Behavior." *American Psychologist,* 1966, *21,* 321–332.

Rozin, P. "The Evolution of Intelligence and Access to the Cognitive Unconscious." In J. M. Sprague and A. N. Epstein (Eds.), *Progress in Psychobiology and Physiological Psychology.* Vol. 6. New York: Academic Press, 1976.

Scarr-Salapatek, S. "Genetics and the Development of Intelligence." In F. Horowitz (Ed.), *Review of Child Development Research.* Vol. 4. Chicago: University of Chicago Press, 1975.

Selfe, L. *Nadia.* London: Academic Press, 1977.

*Scientific American* (Special issue, *The Brain*), September 1980.

Shepard, R. M., and Metzler, J. "Mental Rotation of Three-Dimensional Shapes." *Science,* 1971, *171,* 701–703.

Skinner, B. F. *Science and Human Behavior.* New York: Macmillan, 1953.

Spearman, C. "General Intelligence Objectively Determined and Measured." *American Journal of Psychology,* 1904, *15,* 840–848.

Sperber, D. *Rethinking Symbolism.* New York: Cambridge University Press, 1974.

Suzuki, S. *Nurtured by Love.* New York: Cambridge University Press, 1964.

Taniuchi, L. "The Creation of Prodigies Through Special Early Education: Three Case Studies." Unpublished manuscript, van Leer Project on Human Potential, Harvard Graduate School of Education, Harvard University, 1980.

Thurstone, L. L., and Thurstone, T. G. *Factorial Studies of Intelligence.* Chicago: University of Chicago Press, Psychometric Monographs no. 2, 1941.

Waddington, C. *New Patterns in Genetics and Development.* New York: Columbia University Press, 1962.

Woods, B., and Teuber, H. L. "Changing Patterns of Childhood Aphasia." *Annals of Neurology,* 1978, *3,* 273–280.

*Howard Gardner is codirector, Harvard Project Zero,*
*a neuropsychology researcher at the Boston Veterans'*
*Administration Hospital, and associate professor*
*of neurology in the Boston University School*
*of Medicine.*

*Little is known about the evolving lives of prodigious children,*
*but it often seems to be the case that during adolescence many face*
*a midlife crisis, the outcome of which may determine their chances*
*for later success.*

# Growing Up Prodigies:
# The Midlife Crisis

*Jeanne Bamberger*

A child of six or eight who demonstrates prodigious musical ability is, above all, awe-inspiring. And as with all feelings of awe, there is often an accompanying feeling of fear: Where did this gift come from? How should we as parents, teachers, or neighborhood kids behave with this child? What does he or she know; how did he or she learn to play this Mozart piano concerto so movingly?

In turn, what does it feel like to be a child whose intimates treat him or her with a mixture of awe, fear, and love? What is it like to be singled out, treated as an oddity, "blessed with a gift," and simultaneously asked to carry the burden of its responsibility? What is it like to try and live up to this image? And what is it like to face becoming a grown-up prodigy?

This work was funded in part by grants from the National Institute of Education, the National Science Foundation, and the Ford Foundation. A number of colleagues have contributed to the work reported here. Among these I would like to thank in particular Susan Carey, Carolyn Hildebrandt, Donald A. Schön, and Hermine Sinclair for helping me to clarify the distinctions between figural and formal strategies during the earlier phases of my work, and Lynn Goldsmith for her careful reading and helpful suggestions during the preparation of this chapter. In addition, I am especially grateful to the many individuals who were willing to tell me their own and others' stories of midlife crisis.

D. Feldman (Ed.). *New Directions for Child Development: Developmental Approaches to Giftedness and Creativity,* no. 17.
San Francisco: Jossey-Bass, September 1982.

**61**

62

These are, I believe, some of the questions we need to take very seriously if we are to serve some useful purpose to the fragile evolution of children's lives who demonstrate extraordinary musical ability at an early age. I would like, here, to focus on the last of these questions, which involves the transition from childhood to adulthood, partly because it is a real-life developmental one, and partly because it is, in fact, a question that is vividly and often painfully asked by individuals themselves, even after they have somehow weathered the others. Indeed, the need to confront becoming an adult often signals a critical turning point in the evolving lives of young performers. I have termed this period of painful reappraisal the *midlife crisis*. It seems to occur in the midteens — midlife for those whose public careers may have begun at five or six.

The phenomenon is a surprisingly common one but not much talked about and certainly little studied. This is not surprising, since, at worst, the crisis results in the disappearance from public view of the extraordinary child who had once shown such promise.

One does not ordinarily meet these grown-up prodigies, because they tend to keep their pasts hidden. They carry with them a deep sense of failure, even though they sometimes achieve success in other fields, at least by ordinary standards. But once a sympathetic interest is expressed, the stories begin to emerge and, indeed, to collect. I am personally aware of about a dozen whose stories all share a similar shape. They share a saga of going through a period when their extraordinary musical capacities as performers seem to come apart, to break down. Informants talk about their earlier abilities as a kind of intimate contact with their instruments through which they could bring a piece of music to life. But with this critical period, decisions that were previously made quite spontaneously, directly in terms of actions on their instruments, become problematic, self-conscious, and seemingly without clear direction or resolution. What before were relations that were simply heard, become notes in search of connections. Technical problems simultaneously emerge — it becomes difficult to "get around on the instrument."

While such individuals report that they worked hard, practicing many hours a day, they still, typically, report little understanding of how they did what it was that made them special. Indeed, central to the crisis seems to be the shock of needing to question just what it was they were always before able to do. Most striking, then, is the impression that these young musicians, perhaps for the first time, confront the need to self-consciously reflect on their own understanding — to reflect, for example, on performance decisions that had previously been left unquestioned, spontaneous, "intuitive." Simultaneously, they discover that they have inadequate tools with which to pursue these new questions productively. They talk of trying to learn all over again how to build a relation between their bodies, their instruments, the printed score, and their musical "hearing." They need to learn how to apprehend, to make sense of musical relations all over again. These are, I believe, stories of the struggle involved in the developmental process of transition from childhood prodigiousness to extraordinary, mature excellence.

There are undoubtedly a multitude of factors contributing to this midlife crisis. They include social, emotional, maturational, and professional career issues — doubts and questions concerning fundamental life values. After all, since childhood these prodigies have been singled out, expected to be the best, and asked to live up to these expectations. It is no wonder that, as they approach adulthood, they confront questions of why and what for. Nor is it surprising that there is a great temptation to be absorbed, to become anonymous among ordinary people.

While all of these are crucially important questions, I would like to propose that along with them go specific cognitive issues and that these can be rigorously studied. Further, such cognitive issues are intimately related to those mentioned above through their entangling alliance with reflection. What we may be witnessing here is the powerful effect of seeking to understand, to look *at,* the very means that were previously used to see (and hear) *with.* Such studies could, for example, illuminate crucial differences between childhood prodigiousness and later adult performance. And by thus considering extraordinary ability as an evolving enterprise, we may even shed light on the nature of learning among those children whom we refer to as normal and who, after all, sometimes also become extraordinary adults.

While this is virgin territory, I will try to show that the relevant issues here are related to cognitive developmental concerns that we do know something about. But such study is demanding. It requires, in particular, a deep understanding of music, itself — what we could call the structure of the domain as expressed partly in theoretical knowledge but perhaps more so in a kind of epistemology of expert practice — and, at the same time, a thorough working knowledge of empirical research in cognitive development. The requisite skills are not often combined, understandably, since sophisticated musicians prefer to be just that and cognitive psychologists are rarely expert musicians. To encourage the joining of these enterprises is, in fact, one of the aims of what I will propose here.

## Previous Research

In this section, I will describe previous research carried out primarily by myself and my students. While our previous studies have included adults with no music training, novice musicians (that is, those with only a few years of formal study), and expert professional musicians, our child subjects have included only those with no music training or with only minimal instruction. Still, the results of these studies suggest, I believe, intriguing possibilities for the study of what I have termed midlife crisis. (See Bamberger, 1980, 1981; Bamberger and Schön, 1979.)

The earliest studies were concerned with rhythm — in particular, with the relations between actions, such as clapping back a rhythm, and subjects' descriptions of these actions, such as paper and pencil graphics. The task, as told to the subjects, was to "put on paper something that will help you remember the rhythm tomorrow or so someone else could play it back." Subsequent studies went on to examine the cognitive processes that inform subjects' constructions of melodic coherence.

The results of these studies led to the formulation of two contrasting and distinctive strategies of representation. I have termed these *figural* and *formal*, respectively. The most striking finding was that, while musically naive subjects, both children and adults, tend to focus exclusively on figural aspects of rhythm and pitch relations and musically novice subjects tend to focus exclusively on formal aspects of pitch and time, *it is only expert, professional musicians who are able to understand, make use of, and integrate both kinds of musical relations.*

In general, figural strategies of representation can be distinguished from formal strategies as follows: Figural subjects tend to represent to themselves *groupings* of events into gestures, such as small motives or figures, rather than individual events such as claps or notes. If figural subjects are asked to attend to a singular pitch event, they assign meaning to such an event in relation to its unique situation and function within the figure of which it is a member. Further, figural strategies of representation seem to depend on the immediate sensory experience of bodily actions and the direct juxtaposition of these actions as they occur through space and time. In contrast, purely formal subjects tend to focus on separate, discrete events—that is, on each note individually. Further, they make use of what I have termed *fixed reference structures,* such as the ordered set of pitches in a scale or the hierarchy of metric units generated by specific time and pitch relations. Formal subjects assign meaning to a pitch-time event, then, according to its fixed and invariant position within these reference structures. Unlike figural subjects, formal subjects are able to compare events that are separated or "distanced" in time-space within a melody. They do so by naming, measuring relations, and thus identifying pitch and time properties as same or different in relation to previously internalized fixed reference structures. In turn, they tend to ignore the unique situation or figural function of an event within a particular melody or rhythm.

In order to make these distinctions quite clear, I will describe one kind of experimental situation in some detail. Typically, tasks have involved reconstructing a familiar tune or constructing a tune that the subject likes, using a set of pitch-making objects all of which look the same and can be freely moved about (Montessori bells). Within such task situations, subjects who are characterized as *formal* begin by mapping the mixed array of bells onto a familiar and well-internalized reference structure—that is, they order the bells in a row, with left to right going from low to high in pitch. They then proceed to find the tune *in* or *on* this constructed fixed reference (see Figure 1). Figural subjects, in contrast, build up the tune chronologically. That is, they start by finding a

## Figure 1. "Twinkle, Twinkle Little Star"

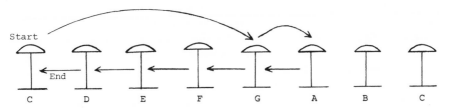

**Formal Reference Structure**

possible first bell-pitch with which to begin the tune, then search for the next, adding it to their cumulative row of bells. They continue, next-next-next, until they have a row of bells whose "path" is the same as that of the tune (see Figure 2). Playing along, straight ahead, on the completed bell path results, then, in an action path that plays the intended tune. We have called these bell paths *one-purpose machines,* since they are intended for and, indeed, are effective for the performance of just one tune. This is in contrast to formal tune builders, who make an *all-purpose machine* — that is, a fixed reference scale, in terms of which many tunes may be found and played.

Formal subjects, must, of course, move forward and backward on their fixed reference scale in order to play the tune, using the same bell as an instantiation of every occurrence of its pitch in a given melody. Further, formal subjects can, through their fixed reference, compare one tune with another, relating each of its (and their) movements to one another through their single, all-purpose machine. Figural subjects, in contrast, will not only build a new bell path for each new tune but, within each bell path, will often use a new object (a new bell) for each pitch event in the tune, not realizing that a later pitch is the same (in pitch property) as one that has already occurred earlier (see Figure 2).

We have given the name *felt path* to these cumulating actions of figural tune builders in their construction of tunes. That is, subjects appear to feel their way along (next-next-next), responding to the results of each action with another, until they have built up a kind of enacted description of the whole. A

## Figure 2. "Twinkle, Twinkle Little Star"

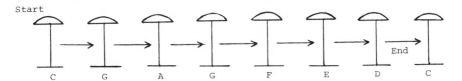

**Figural Bell Path**

felt path, then, becomes a kind of evolving *reference entity:* Through direct actions on objects (bells) and a continuing reflective interaction with their results, vague, often tacit internal strategies shape spatial-temporal external coherence. The outcome of the process is a reference entity in that it functions to hold still progressive actions and decisions made *enroute.*

It is in this sense, then, that figural, felt-path tune builders are said to be necessarily responsive to immediately present context and to the unique function of events along the course of an evolving, felt-path construction. Once an event has passed, it is gone; where you are does not include where you have been: "The past is consumed in the present and the present is living only because it brings forth the future" (Joyce, 1960, p. 251). In contrast, formal tune builders, guided by their internalized reference structures, name and fix the properties of pitch and time in terms of the unique position of such events within these reference structures. As a result, formal subjects can compare and measure events that are separated in time and space through the relating of these events to the reference structure, rather than through the inner functional relations of these events as they occur within the ongoing melody itself.

The distinction between an external reference entity constructed on the spot and a previously acquired and internalized reference structure is crucial here. While a reference structure in the simplest case of a scale can be externalized in spatial, static form (for example, the ordering of the bells from low to high or the ordering of the white keys on the piano keyboard), reference structures in more developed forms are complex, internal mental networks of relations. Such complex mental reference structures are expressible only in symbolic form; or, putting it differently, they give meaning to the conventional symbols associated with practice in the domain.

For example, on the most basic level, the names of pitches or their positions on the staff designate particular places on an instrument. But the names of pitches may also refer, symbolically, to "places" within a mental reference structure along with specifying the distance between them — that is, intervalic pitch relations. Further, the reference structure may assign possible harmonic functions for these pitches within a tonal network, as, for example, tonic or dominant. With more complex reference structures, tonal networks are, themselves, represented in certain relations to one another — that is, a network of networks in which tonalities are thought of and heard as more closely related or more distant. In turn, the same chord (let's say, F-A-C) may play different roles, have a different function in several different tonalities, in this way becoming a common node interconnecting the networks. (For example, F-A-C can be the tonic in the key of F or the dominant in the key of B-flat.) The degree of richness and complexity of internal reference structures strongly determines just what kinds of things and relations an individual can point to or even attend to. Further, internal reference structures strongly influence just what an individual takes to be givens in the domain — what Quine calls an individual's "ontological commitment" (1960).

The strategies for constructing external reference entities are thus quite different in kind from strategies invoked by those who have already acquired and internalized such mental reference structures:

- A reference entity is unique to a particular task — for example, constructing this particular tune
- It exists as a concrete object in space, not as a mental construct
- It functions as a way of holding still found relations
- It serves to define the very terms of the task that only gradually emerge through reflective interaction between players and materials.

The differences between figural and formal strategies as described here could be seen as similar to Piaget's (1960) characterization of earlier and later stages of development. That is, qualities that are associated with the behavior of young children seem to reappear in the figural strategies of older children and even adults when they are confronted with a specific problem in a domain that is new to them. In turn, Piaget's characterization of older children's behavior (concrete operations) seems similar to the strategies of adults with sufficient musical training to read standard music notation (SMN). Concrete operations are "marked, for example, by the point at which temporal relations are merged in the notion of a single time, or the point at which elements of a complex are conceived as constituting an unvarying whole, or the inequalities characterizing a system of relations are serialized in a single scale, and so on" (Piaget, 1960, p. 139).

However, I have argued (Bamberger, 1980) that figural strategies, with their associated reference entities, and formal strategies, with their associated mental reference structures, while responsive to different aspects of music, are both inherent in the structure of even simple rhythms or common tunes as well as much more complex compositions. It is the interaction of these two kinds of relations — unique figural function in contrast to measured time and pitch — that give a rhythm or melody its particular character.

Thus, two events that can be named the same with respect to pitch may sound quite different, depending on their relation to the metric structure in which they occur. Consider, for example, the tune "America":

**Figure 3.**

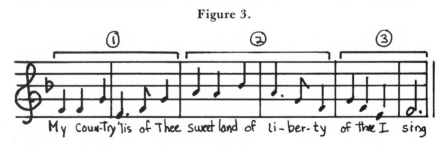

The endings of the first two figures (*thee* and -*ty*) coincide with endings of metric units. But the end of the third figure (*sing*) coincides with the *beginning* of a metric unit. The differences in the interaction between figural boundaries and metric boundaries here influence the feeling of the events that mark figural endings: The first two figures, seemingly paradoxically, feel less ended when they coincide with metric endings; the third figure feels more ended because it coincides with a metric beginning. But it so happens that the second and third figures end on the same pitch! This same pitch functions differently and is sung differently in each situation as a result of its position in the metric structure (this, along with differences in the duration of each, how it is approached, and so forth). Thus, if you were to say that these two events were not the same, you would be right in every respect except pitch. But, if you were a figural listener, you might well say they were different in pitch as well. You would be responding to the global feel of the events, as a result of all these interacting dimensions. If you were a formal listener, you might respond in terms of your internalized reference structure through which you could place, name, and hold steady the invariant pitch property of the two events, separating pitch from the various other dimensions that determine their unique figural functions. Thus, to identify these two events as the same would be to focus on just one dimension and to set aside the others that give these events their particular, situational meanings and their particular feelings.

It seems, then, that you need to be able to do both—that is, place and measure and, in addition, respond to interacting dimensions as these generate unique, figural functions. Indeed, I would argue that it is the continuing development of transactions between figural and formal strategies of representation that is necessary to what could be termed fully developed musicality.

The problem is that, while musicians do use figural strategies, they tend to do so tacitly. Figural strategies, for example, often account for what musicians refer to as "playing musically," or "actively shaping a phrase," or even "playing with feeling." But figural strategies that help to guide musical performance and even musical apprehension (as expressed in the phrase "having a musical ear") are seen to be spontaneous, on-the-spot moves between the performer-listener and the music that he or she is shaping. Understandably, this leaves such figural strategies mysterious, magical, labeled intuitive, attributed to innate talent, and even valued as such. To probe for their cognitive underpinnings is, in turn, often taken to be if not impossible, at least immoral. It is as if figural and formal ways of understanding and constructing coherence were opaque to one another—the first mysterious and indescribable, the second supposedly objective and uniformly expressible in a symbolic notation.

It follows from these findings that the traditional view of developmental change (for example, stages of development) should not be seen as simply a linear progression, at least in the musical domain: Figural strategies should not be seen as something to go beyond, to overcome, to be replaced by those representations that characterize formal thought. Rather, I would argue, it is the interacting evolution between two complementary ways of understanding, each enriching the other, that characterizes fully developed musical intelligence. Thus, I have concluded from these studies that what may well characterize the expert listener-performer is the capacity to retain and play with the tension between formal understanding, where the focus is on the *invariant* particularity of pitch and time properties with respect to fixed reference structures, and figural ways of understanding, where the response is to the particularity of an event resulting from its contextually embedded function in a unique reference entity.

## Implications for Midlife Crisis

In this section, I return to the evolving lives of extraordinary young musicians and to my opening questions. To them I now add: What are the implications of the distinctions between figural and formal strategies of representation in accounting for the breakdown of prodigious capacities during midadolescence? My speculations (and they can be no more than that) will rest on the following arguments:

- An integration of figural and formal strategies of representation is necessary to fully developed musical intelligence — that is, mature artistry
- Prodigious musical ability can be seen as an expression of extraordinarily highly developed figural strategies for representing and constructing musical coherence
- Formal constructions and associated mental reference structures are, for musical prodigies, relatively impoverished, separate from, and even incongruent with their operative figural strategies
- The breakdown of musical capacities results, at least in part, from the need to confront these incongruences
- In order for effective integration to take place, both figural and formal strategies of representation must undergo development and change
- If such development and change does occur, it is precipitated by the individual's courage and determination to search for effective tools with which to reflect on musical understanding in the face of pervasive doubts concerning most of life's fundamental values, including musical ones.

In describing her passage through disarray, one of my informants said, "It was as if I had to be inside and outside at the same time." What did she mean? Consider the following possible scenario: Early prodigious performance is the expression of abnormally highly developed, extraordinary figural capacities. Closely linked to action (like the "smart fingers" of a talented mechanic), apprehension is through the intimacy of instrument and hand; a passage, even an entire composition, is internalized, memorized, as a particular felt path, a kinesthetically encoded sequence of actions with each action-figure calling up and entraining the next. What exists for these performers is immediately present coherence along this path; comparisons across figures, more global coherence are elusive. Formal aspects of musical coherence are familiar — the score, units of analysis associated with music theory — but these are about something else, separate, outside of the operative, action-based, inside representation of a piece. To reinforce, emphasis in teaching is on the development of technical skills — that is, action knowledge; musical decisions (phrasing, dynamics, even fingering) are proscribed, given beforehand, or acquired by imitating the teacher's example. The result is that, while exhibiting extraordinary capacities for realizing a composition, young performers acquire only limited means for externalizing, reflecting on, thinking about what they know how to do so well. Why should it be otherwise?

Because there comes an emerging need in midadolescence to ask why, to find out for themselves, to take responsibility for their own decisions, their own learning and making of coherence. Growing up prodigies find themselves at a loss, without adequate tools for making the move into going it alone. Before, a score encountered for the first time was simply a set of directions, transparent to actions, a map for where the fingers should go. In the flux of pervasive doubts and with the need for personal independence and understanding, the score becomes something to look *at* — a possible source of answers but also a source of puzzlement, a code to be interpreted in order to find and construct an apprehended coherence that can guide actions. In short, the adolescent's need to reflect results, at first, in chaos. The current state of figural knowledge is open to question but is as yet left uninformed, untouched by the more formal relations that can be named, measured, fixed. What used to be is in disarray; what can be described and looked at answers different questions. The objects of figural representation and the objects of formal representation have no common ground. How, then, can one be "inside and outside at the same time"?

The struggle becomes one of building new entities that will converge in a single "ontological commitment." In the figural, felt-path representations of childhood, musical dimensions were productively fused in reciprocal interaction forming unique, structural functions and feelings projected at one particular moment. In the face of reflective questioning, however, fused dimensions and figural groupings come apart into starkly separate properties. And with analysis, felt paths break apart, too: A figure approached from one direction is recognized as the figure previously approached from another. But, as in coming upon a familiar landmark in a new way, the conjunction of familiarity with strangeness is, at first, disorienting. Then, as with the two places, the two figures become one, gaining new meaning as they become embedded in a more complete network that can include them both. A passage that was understood to be, and played as if it were, something new, is discovered to be a "return" —

albeit transfigured—to the very opening of the piece. A new coherence is constructed, now on a more global level. At the same time, the idea, *return,* as an object symbolically represented in mental reference structures, is expanded; *return* may be the result of all that has gone before and is thus transfigured, not merely the same thing once again.

In this way, a particular event, dependent for its meaning on the unique reference entity in which it occurs, begins to influence formal reference structures: The limited specificity of formal objects expands to include more complex networks of relations. The scale as a representation of a tonality expands to include a network of interrelated functions. These dynamic relations, in turn, illuminate unique moments in a specific piece at a specific moment. The generating of a tonality by the particular confluence of metric accent and pitch intervals may be made congruent with kinesthetically represented "handing," a surprising sonority that was before unexplained may be realized as an unexpected harmonic function; a return may be performed with a different gesture. Concretely experienced, unique reference entities are informed by (and, in turn, reciprocally inform) reference structures. The very notions of *same* and *different* are transformed, and with them, their apprehension in real time. Out of a struggle for reason may, perhaps, come a transforming evolution where inside and outside, figural and formal, converge. As Wolff points out in *The Teaching of Artur Schnabel* (1972): "The mature performer works for those rare inspirations when his conception of the score becomes one with its physical realization in performance. At such moments, technique is more than just the disciplined functioning of the body at the command of the ear: It grows into a physical activity which in turn may stimulate the imagination. As Schnabel put it, 'If all goes well, the conception materializes and the materialization redissolves into conception'" (p. 22). This is, I believe, one story of the passage from childhood prodigiousness to mature, independent artistry.

But the scenario I have proposed must be only part of the story. Inasmuch as musical-cognitive factors contribute to this period of chaos, they do so only as a single thread in the complex fabric of the evolving lives of growing up prodigies. I want to suggest, however, that the issues raised in this story, the tensions and incongruences between figural and formal strategies of representation and the struggle to redefine the entities and relations associated with them, mirror those that characterize other aspects of this tangled web—that is, personal, interpersonal, and even maturational factors.

While I can only posit these interconnections here, they suggest the need for bringing together fields of study that have largely remained isolated from one another. For example, psychoanalytically oriented literature, along with biography and autobiography, abounds with accounts of personal crises of midadolescence. But little attempt has been made to connect these with the cognitive, domain-specific factors that I have tried to focus on.

What seems to unite all aspects of midadolescent life is the search for independent identity. With it, self-conscious awareness of fundamental assumptions emerges, coupled with the need for means with which productively to disentangle, reflect on, and reconstruct in a new way capacities, values, and ways of seeing that before had been taken for granted: "We are thus most aware of our identity when we are just about to gain it, and when we (with that specific startle which motion pictures call a 'double take') are somewhat surprised to make its acquaintance; or again when we are just about to enter a crisis and feel the encroachment of identity confusion" (Erikson, 1968, p. 165).

For growing up prodigies, children who have since childhood been in public view, the rocky path toward independence seems fraught with special tensions. My informants each tell of a childhood in which they were singled out, isolated from their peers but at the same time made dependent by the intimate care and guidance of mentors—teachers, parents—and a self-image acquired through them. They tell of the need to succeed now in their own terms—along with a fear of ignominious failure—the feeling of being abandoned ("kicked out," as one informant put it) and simultaneously wanting to abandon—to find musical and personal identity of their own—and the desire to stand apart, separate and unique, special, while at the same time seeking ways to join with others or even *one* other:

> His thinking was a dust of doubt and self-mistrust, lit up at moments by the lightenings of intuition, but lightenings of so clear a splendor that in those moments the world perished about his feet as if it had been fire consumed: And thereafter his tongue grew heavy and he met the eyes of others with unanswering eyes, for he felt that the spirit of beauty had folded him round like a mantle and that in reverie at least he had been acquainted with nobility. But, when this brief pride of silence upheld him no longer, he was glad to find himself still in the midst of common lives, passing on his way amid the squalor and noise and sloth of the city fearlessly and with a light heart (Joyce, 1960, pp. 176–177).

The merging of social, personal, and career issues with the specifically musical concerns discussed earlier in this chapter is perhaps most clearly reflected in the need for productive means with which to reason and reflect—to take apart feelings, even entities (figures) that before seemed inviolable, to regroup, and to justify. At the same time, there is the sense that available intellectual tools given from the "outside"—words that name, measure, and assign value, theories that analyze—are incongruent with, unable to explain, disconnected from spontaneous inner needs and capacities such as immediately present, sentient feelings and actions. "He found himself glancing from one casual word to another on his right and left in stolid wonder that they had been so silently emptied on instantaneous sense until every mean shop legend bound his mind like the words of a spell and his soul shriveled up sighing with age as he walked on in a lane among heaps of dead language" (Joyce, 1960, p. 178). The image that comes to mind is a window that one has always looked *through* and that gave shape and coherence to objects and relations — transparent to action. At this critical turning point, the window becomes something to look *at*. But in all its fine-grained detail, it reflects different entities, answers different questions.

Future resolution can be neither a return to what was nor a simple "fix-up." As in other creative acts, the process is one of evolution and transformation, of almost literally coming to see in a new way. And as Gruber (1981) has pointed out with respect to new insight in science, the apparent moment of insight is more often a culmination of just such internally worked over mutual transformations of both inner and outer ways of knowing and seeing. What I have characterized as the figural-formal transaction is, I believe, one way that such evolutions or revolutions take place.

## Conclusions

I have tried to conjoin in this chapter the results of empirical research and the stories of extraordinary young musicians as a way of explicating some aspects of the critical passage from musical prodigiousness to adult artistry. From the research, I have argued that the coherence-making structures of music are, themselves, dependent on an interaction between qualitatively different kinds of relations: those I have called figural, dependent on the unique situation of an event within a passage where it occurs; and those I have called formal, instantiations of properties and procedures common to much of the music of our culture, usually expressed in the symbolisms of notation and theory. I have concluded that it is the capacity to make use of, understand, and integrate both figural and formal aspects of musical coherence that characterizes fully developed musical intelligence (Bamberger, 1981; Bamberger and Schön, 1979).

In turn, I have suggested that those who demonstrate extraordinary musical ability as children are expressing extraordinary figural capacities in their internal representations and performance of music. This includes remarkably highly developed capacities for apprehending and projecting musical coherence and feelings through their body sense in relation to their instrument — that is, what I have called felt path representations.

I have also proposed that chaos, and even the breakdown of early capacities is at least influenced by the adolescent's emerging need to reflect on what he or she has until how taken for granted. This need leads to a confrontation between figural understandings that have worked so well in the past and formal understandings as expressed symbolically in notations and other categories of analysis. Through this initial confrontation, the units of perception and action associated with figural strategies come apart, but the units of analysis that name, measure, and fix seem inappropriate to building a new coherence. I have argued, however, that if an individual can face the risk of confronting the incongruences between these two ways of knowing that have tended to remain opaque to one another, the entities and relations characterizing each may mutually transform. The result is the possibility for making *multiple representations*. This means developing the possibility of focusing now on one aspect of a passage, now on another, experimenting with and making choices between possible and even impossible interpretations or, as musicians like to say, hearing a passage first one way then another as attention is shifted among and across dimensions. Artur Schnabel embodied this process in his belief that "Practicing was experiment rather than drill" (Wolff, 1972, p. 173).

It follows from this account that, when a musically prodigious child plays, for example, a Mozart violin concerto, he or she is internally representing that composition in a way quite different from what he or she will do as an adult artist. At the same time, it follows that we must distinguish between precocious and prodigious musical abilities: The child who plays so movingly that one is "brought to tears" is doing so not in a way that others will achieve at a later age but doing so in a way that others will rarely, if ever, achieve at all!

Finally, I have tried to suggest that midlife crisis is the result of a confluence of factors, interrelated in their expression of a need for independent identity. I have taken this to mean a quest for means with which to reflect productively on music-making decisions as well as decisions relating to social, personal, and professional commitments, values, and ideologies, such that ways of knowing can coexist in mutual transaction. As Erikson describes it (1968): "An optimal sense of identity . . . is experienced merely as a sense of psychosocial well-being. Its most obvious concomitants are a feeling of being at home in one's body, a sense of 'knowing where one is going,' and an inner assuredness of anticipated recognition from those who count" (p. 165).

## Implications for Future Research

In my initial comments, I urged that research be directed toward real world, useful purposes. In that spirit, now, I would like to suggest three areas of potential study.

First, experiments designed to provide insight into the transformations in internal representation that may occur as children move from early prodigious ability to adult artistry. Such studies might also explicate further the distinctions between figural and formal strategies of representation, as well as their changing role in the course of musical development.

Can we, for example, tease apart the influence of age in contrast to that of training? Consider, for instance, bell tasks similar to those described earlier in the chapter. Will young children who read music and are already acclaimed performers use felt path strategies to build a reference entity (as would their untrained peers), thus reflecting hypothesized figural representations? Will they build a reference structure reflecting more formal internal representation? Or will their behavior suggest conflicts in strategies when they are thrust into this unfamiliar musical medium? Will older subjects behave in significantly different ways from young children?

Can we devise experimental situations to study the interactions between "body feel" and symbolic descriptions at different ages? Subjects might be asked, for instance, to work in an environment where they are once removed from a kinesthetic relation to an instrument and where the notation system is analogous but different from standard notation. Consider, here, an interactive computer-generated music environment in which pitch and time relations are played as a result of subjects' purely symbolic input. In addition, the referents of the notation system are at a different level of analysis — for example, figures instead of notes. If subjects are asked, then, to make a coherent melody built up from varying sets of melodic figures (small, structural entities), will we observe significant differences among subjects at different ages — differences in the construction strategies they use, in the tunes they build, in the kinds of difficulties they confront? Will we be able to relate these differences to aspects of figural-formal strategies of representation? (See Bamberger, 1977.)

I would propose, particularly, that experimental situations be designed so as to lead subjects into a mode of active experimentation. It is my argument here that we will gain useful insights into shifts in mental representation through close observations of subjects in action — that is, as they work in task situations where they are asked to actually *make* coherent musical objects in contrast to being asked for simple, verbal responses within the constraints of ready-made stimuli. At best, such tasks would encourage subjects actually to learn. In turn, the subjects' current capacities to learn will best demonstrate the limits of their implicit "theories" of the domain as well as their capacities for transformations in representation. Observation and analysis in these dynamic situations may well teach us the most about these extraordinary individuals; and through such studies we may even find better ways to ease the trajectory through midlife crises.

A second group of studies might focus specifically on the period of midlife crisis. Here, a series of in-depth case studies would seem appropriate. Cases might include individuals who passed through this critical period successfully as well as those who failed to do so. This work would necessarily involve researchers from disciplines that usually remain isolated from one another — clinicians, developmental-cognitive psychologists, as well as professional musicians. A primary concern would be to gain insight into the interactions between those particular emotional, interpersonal, maturational, and cognitive-musical factors that contribute to this period of flux and disarray.

Finally, I would propose research having to do specifically with teaching. Such studies are both more difficult to imagine and more problematic because of their tampering effect. Two sorts of directions, however, are worth trying.

First, potentially interesting phenomena might be generated by videotaping and analyzing actual student-teacher interactions during lessons. We might imagine, for example, developing a kind of typology of kinds of instruction — for instance, those concerning technical skills ("Hold the bow closer to the frog," "Lower your wrist when passing your thumb under"); those that suggest a mood or character to the student ("Think of yourself as just floating on a cloud here," "This passage needs to be played with real tenderness"); and especially those that point toward helping the student view technical tools as means towards expressive feeling ("To make that spot sound more lively, change your bow on the third beat"). It would be important in the analysis to look for a developing repertoire of learning strategies that the teacher is helping the student to internalize — that is, situations to which the student can apply similar strategies. What, indeed is the nature of his or her developing ontological commitment? What are the "things" that make up the performer's universe?

From these studies a second, more challenging group of studies might emerge. These would seek to develop means for helping students reflect on their own practice more effectively, both in the sense of their day-to-day work (practicing) and also in the sense of the practice of their profession. It would be important to find approaches that bring felt path, figural representations into closer relation with symbolically represented reference structures. Such research would necessarily involve serious studies in music theory. The purpose of such studies would be to develop modes of description that are more dynamic, more process-oriented and kinesthetic in their orientation towards musical structure itself; this, of course, in the service of anticipating and allaying figural-formal confrontations that, as I have suggested, may contribute to the midlife crisis.

It should be obvious that any of these proposals requires, above all, removing the barriers that have traditionally separated researchers both within related disciplines as well as across disciplines. Thus, it would seem imperative to recruit and train a new, interdisciplinary cadre of researchers dedicated to the study of real world issues in the evolving lives of extraordinarily gifted musicians. In this way we might at least imagine a "network of enterprise" that would lend support and courage to growing up prodigies as they face the "dust and doubt of self-mistrust" that seems inevitably to accompany the evolution from youthful promise to adult artistry and even beyond. . .

## References

Bamberger, J. "In Search of a Tune." In D. Perkins and B. Leondar (Eds.), *The Arts and Cognition.* Baltimore, Md.: Johns Hopkins University Press, 1977.

Bamberger, J. "Cognitive Structuring in the Apprehension and Description of Simple Rhythms." *Archives de Psychologie,* 1980, *48,* 171–199.

Bamberger, J. "Revisiting Children's Descriptions of Simple Rhythms." In S. Strauss (Ed.), *U-Shaped Behavioral Growth.* New York: Academic Press, 1981.

Bamberger, J., and Schön, D. A. "The Figural-Formal Transaction." Division for Study and Research in Education, M.I.T., Working Paper no. 1, 1979.

Erikson, E. *Identity, Youth, and Crisis.* New York: Norton, 1968.

Gruber, H. E. *Darwin on Man.* Chicago: University of Chicago Press, 1981.

Joyce, J. *A Portrait of the Artist as a Young Man.* New York: Viking, 1960.

Piaget, J. *The Psychology of Intelligence.* Totowa, N.J.: Littlefield, Adams, 1960.
Quine, W. V. *Word and Object.* Cambridge, Mass.: M.I.T. Press, 1960.
Wolff, K. *The Teaching of Artur Schnabel.* New York: Praeger, 1972.

*Jeanne Bamberger is associate professor of Education and Music in the Division for Study and Research in Education at M.I.T. Her research is concerned primarily with cognitive aspects of musical development and learning and how these relate to intellectual growth in other domains of knowledge.*

*For children who exhibit extreme academic promise, one response is to provide radical early acceleration into college. As with all other solutions, however, this one represents a series of compromises.*

# The Optimal Match: Devising the Best Compromise for the Highly Gifted Student

Nancy M. Robinson
Halbert B. Robinson

Providing an optimal educational setting for the highly able learner requires multiple compromises. The educational system in contemporary United States is an age-graded progression that allows little flexibility for the youngster who is different. For the very bright child, it is impossible within the system to achieve, simultaneously, matching with classmates who are (1) of the same age and average intelligence, (2) at the child's own level of social and emotional maturity, and (3) at the child's level of intellectual maturity and/or academic achievement. Placement in segregated classes for gifted youngsters precludes interaction with nongifted peers and, for the highly advanced child, may still not provide an adequate match in other spheres. Acceleration of academic placement (grade skipping) can often improve the match between capability and intellectual challenge and provide exposure to a wider range of non-

The work cited was supported in part by grants from the Ford Foundation, the Spencer Foundation, and the U.S. Office of Education. Thanks are due to Paul Janos, Judy Opacki, Charles Stillman, and other members of the Child Development Research Group.

D. Feldman (Ed.). *New Directions for Child Development: Developmental Approaches to Giftedness and Creativity,* no. 17. San Francisco: Jossey-Bass, September 1982.

gifted young people, but it may throw the gifted youngster into a social setting demanding more maturity than he or she has achieved. Retaining the child in the grade indicated by his or her age, with pullout classes and out of school activities for enrichment, requires the least involvement by school personnel but may relegate the child to five or six miserable hours each day. Choosing the appropriate compromise and making it work constitutes a potent challenge for students, parents, teachers, and counselors.

The major portion of this chapter is devoted to a description of one such compromise, a radical acceleration program for highly able students who are intellectually and academically prepared for work at the university level long before they are of the ordinary age to enter college. The Early Entrance Program at the University of Washington, since its inception in 1977, has accepted students who have essentially outgrown high school while still in junior high. A radical acceleration program for the student who is radically different from his or her peers, it is founded on the assumption that, for a substantial proportion of students, priority should be given to the match between learner and the intellectual challenge.

## Competing Assumptions About the Education of Gifted Youth

Before proceeding to describe the Early Entrance Program, however, it might be well to expand our consideration of the reasons why compromises, rather than perfect solutions, are the best we can hope for, given a highly gifted student in an age-graded system. In so doing, we need to examine some of our most basic beliefs about child development and education. The fact is that most of us hold a series of assumptions that need to be prioritized, if we are not to be immobilized by equally compelling, incompatible alternatives.

### Assumptions About Learning

A set of basic truisms about learning constitutes the first set of assumptions:

1. Learning is a sequential, developmental process that is relatively predictable. One can, then, assess a student's progress in attaining orderly sets of concepts and skills.

2. Once a learner has mastered a given stage or level of skills and conceptual understanding, it is time to proceed to the next. If moving on to the next step is delayed, boredom will ensue; if it occurs too fast, the learner will be confused and discouraged. This is essentially what Hunt meant by the *match* which refers in Piagetian theory to the principle that learning occurs only when there is "an appropriate match between the circumstances that a child encounters and the schemata that he [or she] has already assimilated into his [or her] repertoire" (Hunt, 1961, p. 268). This principle tends to argue against enrichment programs that aim to expand the knowledge base of the student without moving to increased levels of complexity and challenge.

3. Among children of a given age who have been afforded a standard school curriculum, there are substantial differences in learning status that primarily reflect differences in rate of learning. Individual differences characterize not only overall cognitive development (that is, general intelligence) but also specific subject areas and skills; there are also intraindividual differences that must be taken into account.

With respect to these assumptions alone, it should be possible to devise appropriate educational programs without compromise. Individually paced curricula such as self-teaching programs (which, alas, in practice seldom produce much enthusiasm or insight) or a flexible assignment system in which learners are matched to incremental classes in specific subject areas should do the trick. Unfortunately, however, we simultaneously hold other sets of assumptions that complicate the situation.

### Assumptions Favoring an Age-Graded System

Classes in the United States today are organized by age of pupils and deviations from age norm are disapproved. Children who are slow learners are socially promoted until they become such dismal failures that special placement becomes necessary. Exceptionally precocious children move nominally at the very same pace, one grade per year. Even special programs for gifted and retarded children advance one grade designation per year. To be sure, many teachers try to individualize instruction, to teach prescriptively, and to accommodate to the different learning rates of their pupils. Some create smaller subgroups within the classroom and encourage students to do special projects and to study more advanced texts on their own. Special self-contained and pull-out programs usually focus on horizontal enrichment, although some advancement is unavoidable. Such adjustments tend to be piecemeal and uncoordinated, however, increasing the problems of the child who has already mastered a subject before he or she is the "right age" for it.

This rigid adherence to age-grade correspondence is relatively new in American education, a product of the post World War II era and its egalitarian ideals. Prior to that time, one often found a mixture of ages represented in classrooms because of grade skipping *(double promotion)* and holding back (Kett, 1974). Most of the gifted children in Terman's study (Terman and Oden, 1947) were accelerated one or more grade levels in school. Even today we encourage excellence and advancement in the performing arts and athletics. Who has said that a teenage champion swimmer should be held back from the Olympics because of being too young?

The rationale opposed to flexibility in grade placement as a means of meeting the needs of the intellectually advanced student rests in part on educational concerns, in part on concern for the social adjustment of the child, and in part on our current concept of the "American Way." There has been particular concern about any academic program that smack of elitism, especially programs that tend to involve more children from middle-class families than from families less well situated. Programs that increase rather than decrease social imbalance are similarly antithetical to the thrust of social equalization. Unfortunately, school aptitude, at this point in our nation's history at least, is in fact correlated with social, educational, and economic status of parents. This fact runs counter to the state of affairs we would wish — giftedness, in our ideal world, being independent of family background — and restricts our latitude of decision making.

Within the context of this social outlook, there lie strong concerns. It would be well, then, to examine some educational and developmental assumptions that bolster the age-grade system and require the compromises mentioned earlier: The reason most often advanced for the age-grade system is that advancement according to educational achievement ignores the students' maturity in social and emotional spheres. Such maturity is thought to correspond rather specifically to chronological age (see, for example, Gold, 1965; Rothman and Levine, 1963), and it is argued, therefore, that academic advancement may jeopardize healthy progress in other areas (Congdon, 1979).

There is, to be sure, a lack of sufficient data in this area, but there is available considerable evidence to challenge the specificity of age and maturity level. We know, for example, that during the middle school years, girls on the whole tend to be more mature both physically and heterosexually than boys, and we know in addition that measures of intelligence and social competence show a strong positive relationship (Hurst, 1962; Meyers, Nihira, and Zetlin, 1979), as do intelligence and social reasoning (Greenspan, 1979). With the expected publication in 1983 of the revised Vineland Scale, one can predict a spate of studies focused upon social maturity (and, it is to be hoped, on individual differences).

A wealth of publications deal with academic advancement of bright students, including early admission to kindergraten or first grade, grade skipping, advanced placement courses for college credit, and early admission to college. These studies strongly suggest that such practices benefit those who are allowed to move ahead according to their competencies (Daurio, 1979; Gallagher, 1975; Newland, 1976). As Keating has observed with respect to acceleration, "As for the socioemotional concerns, it seems time to abandon them unless and until some solid reliable evidence is forthcoming that indicates real dangers in well-run programs" (1979, p. 218).

A second reason given for adhering to the age-grade system is the importance of academic content provided at each grade level. Grade skipping causes students to miss important learning experiences (see, for example, Hildreth, 1966). Such gaps are not limited to grade skipping. Indeed, because each of the states adopts its own curriculum guidelines, gaps are often created for average as well as gifted students whose families move about the country. In fact, these gaps are much more likely to pass unnoticed than those created by skipping, because they have been created inadvertently. The arguments for a coherent and well-planned curriculum are justified. Concepts, skills, and essential specific facts may be omitted when grades are skipped. Even so, there is little evidence to indicate that bright students who skip are handicapped (Keating, 1976; Stanley, Keating, and Fox, 1974). Specific gaps in sequential areas can be handled directly, and material in nonsequential subjects that is repeated, spiral fashion, several times during one's school career, can be acquired at subsequent grade levels as well as through college work and independent study.

Similarly, there is concern for the omission of nonacademic experiences and extracurricular activities of the school years. Class offices, school newspaper and yearbook, and team sports are regarded as valuable preparation for adult life. Of course, students who are young for grade are unlikely to be the football heroes of their class, but they may well edit newspapers, take photographs for the yearbook, serve as coxswain for the crew, enter the marching band, participate in a debate club, or play the ingenue in the school play. The evidence does not suggest that age per se strongly affects participation in extracurricular activities. In fact, in a study of high school students who had been admitted to kindergarten at an early age, Hobson (1963) found the underage students actually engaged in a significantly larger average number of extracurricular activities including athletic and social honors, elective offices, and awards at graduation.

A "simple" solution has seemed feasible: Individualized instruction has been advanced as the answer to meeting the needs of diverse children of the same age. The classroom teacher is thought capable of providing for differences in performance levels both between children and within the same child. Paradoxically, this is in some ways a much easier task when the child is moving slowly through the curriculum than when he or she is moving rapidly, for the duller child uses up lesson plans at a much slower rate. With bright pupils, the classroom teacher often simply can not keep up. If an enrichment program is provided by a special teacher, it in turn must provide for differences in rates of learning or the very advanced gifted child will again be seriously underchallenged.

A number of other arguments have been advanced to support the age-grade system. It is argued, for example, that cognitive advancement may not be stable; the child who is far ahead at one age may not be at another. While this may occur in some instances, most longitudinal studies of children identified at school age indicate a strong correlation between earlier and later intellectual measures. (Several parents of entering kindergartners from different school districts have reported to us conversations with school principals whose remarks have been to this effect: "Even if your little darling has been reading for two or three years, by the time we get him or her to third grade, he or she won't be different from any of the others.") Some studies suggest that young people can be robbed of a carefree childhood and "burn out" at an early age; others fear that accelerating the highest achieving students will deprive nongifted age peers of valuable role models (though these same students can provide role models wherever they are); still others are concerned about the negative effects of letting a child know he or she is gifted (as if such a characteristic were a blot on the family). Finally, it is said to be unfair to allow youngsters to leave school before graduation at age eighteen, implying that school is a sentence to be served for bad behavior.

## Assumptions Favoring a Competency-Based System

We have already examined assumptions about learning and individual differences favoring a system that provides a challenge to the able learner and permits advancement to the extent that it is appropriate to the student. We have also reviewed the assumptions that contraindicate acceleration as a viable compromise for gifted students and support the age-grade structure of the educational establishment. Admittedly, for both sets of assumptions the empirical evidence is scanty, particularly when one inquires about long-range consequences.

We have also previously quoted comprehensive reviews of the literature, of which Daurio (1979) is the most thorough and up to date, in support of the conclusion that carefully selected students are likely to profit, rather than suffer, from a program that provides carefully monitored acceleration. Before describing one such program, let us examine a final set of assumptions that tend to tip the scales in favor of making available as one option or one compromise advancement that is greater than one grade per year.

Precocious children in an age-graded system often become bored and frustrated (Hollingworth, 1942; Newland, 1976; Terman, 1925), sometimes tuning out and turning off, sometimes misbehaving. What were once eager learners become disenchanted, uncurious, often angry or withdrawn, seat fillers. The child who finishes early the assignment he or she could have done several years ago, who finds the teacher's careful presentations obvious and elementary, is forced to waste precious time and to find some means to adapt to the classroom scene. Such adaptations are not likely to be positive ones.

A serious outcome of the situation described here is that gifted children are seldom encouraged to develop habits of organization, self-discipline, or persistence in the face of adversity. When every classroom problem seems self-evident, when all one's homework can be completed easily during school hours, and when one's offhand effort is better than the laborious product of another child, a set of expectations about the world is developed that undermines one when a true challenge is presented. Frequently, when such youngsters encounter a program for gifted children or finally enter a selective college they become anxious and discouraged. When they must exert an effort to learn or to produce a paper, they think that something is wrong with them and find the whole situation aversive rather than intriguing. While a student of lesser talents who is accustomed to an occasional failure could pick up the pieces and proceed, these children panic, adopt avoidance mechanisms (such as not going to class or delaying the assignment), and further complicate their situations, sometimes withdrawing from school altogether.

Although empirical studies about the peer relationships of academically gifted students are surprisingly few, there is a trend in the data that suggests that the positive social adjustment of the young, gifted child may worsen during the middle school, early adolescent years, with girls perhaps suffering more than boys a decline in social status and a devaluation of intellectual attainments (Austin and Draper, 1981). The process seems to proceed downhill for gifted adolescent girls, though boys may regain their favorable status during the latter years of high school. Presumably, the youngster who is intellectually advanced is rejected as different from the rest, perhaps viewed as somewhat threatening or distant.

At the extreme, some proportion of gifted children become unmistakable isolates among their age peers; this is particularly frequent with students who are extraordinarily precocious (Terman, 1925, Hollingworth, 1942). Rather than profiting from the opportunities available — the athletic teams, class offices, and marching bands — they may be regarded by others and may regard themselves as misfits. This maladaptive pattern is often used as evidence that the student should not be moved ahead in school. "Why," it is said, "he or she cannot even get along with children of the same age. How could he or she succeed with older children?" And yet, many gifted children, as we know, on their own seek out older children as companions (Painter, 1976; Freeman, 1979).

Finally, it can be argued that a school plan that advances children according to competence can be run less expensively than a program that requires either extensive individualized curriculum planning on the part of the regular classroom teacher or a special pull-out class and special materials. The chief ingredient in a competency-based system becomes the school psychologist or counselor who can match child to class(es) and vice versa — a matchmaker, literally and figuratively.

This brief overview has touched only the superficial, gliding rapidly over real concerns voiced by parents, teachers, and students about how best to go about meeting the needs of academically talented youngsters. It has been meant to convey not the simplicity but the complexity of the decisions that must be made about individual children. One must take into account not only the child's intellectual power and preparation but factors such as social, emotional, and physical maturity (which may not be in synchrony with each other). The pleasures being reaped (or not reaped) from nonacademic aspects of the school situation, available out of school activities that may enrich and challenge the child's best efforts, the alternatives within the school (or the family's available choices of schools) — all must be reckoned with. For any given child, it will be almost impossible to find a school setting that optimizes every aspect of the situation, particularly if the child is not merely moderately gifted but extraordinarily so. The right compromise for one child may well not be right for another. Priorities will have to be chosen and experiments tried.

## The University of Washington's Early Entrance Program

As part of a comprehensive program to investigate aspects of intellectual precocity and devise ways to meet the needs of highly gifted young students, the Early Entrance Program was established in 1977 by Halbert B. Robinson and his colleagues in the University of Washington's Child Development Research Group. Already under their auspices was a longitudinal study of highly precocious children identified during the preschool years; from that study had grown a preschool devoted to gifted children and a diagnostic and counseling service. As the outgrowth of consultation and collaboration between the Child Development Research Group and the Seattle School District, a public school individual progress program (IPP) had also been established to serve students performing four or more grade levels in advance of their age mates. Faced with the future prospect of graduates from the IPP who would still be in their early teens, Robinson devised a program to enable highly gifted youngsters to enter the university as qualified regular students.

The Early Entrance Program was, of course, not the first program to facilitate the entry of young students into a university. Indeed, at almost any moderately large or large university, one will find one or more significantly underage students upon whom a kindly admissions officer has taken pity. Other programs of early entry exist at the University of Chicago and elsewhere, but currently the largest and best established program is that at Johns Hopkins University under the leadership of Julian Stanley. Indeed, the programs have much in common although they also have their distinctive differences (Robinson, forthcoming).

Although the Early Entrance Program has from time to time accepted a few students as transfers from high school — some because they were clearly qualified for university work two or three years early, some because they were clearly making a mess of their high school careers despite their very high ability — it is the *radical accelerants* who form the major substance of the program. These students, qualifying for admission by the age of fourteen, have attained scores on the Washington PreCollege Test (a test like the SAT given in Washington State) at or above the ninetieth percentile on either the verbal or quantitative composite and at or above the fiftieth percentile on the other. The norms with which the applicants are compared are high school juniors and seniors who subsequently enter four-year colleges. The applicants are on a competitive footing with other freshmen in academic prowess. In addition, the students must demonstrate an outstanding scholastic record, be recommended by at least some of their teachers or counselors, and demonstrate a high level of motivation to attempt the program. The youngest to qualify was ten-years-old at the time. Table 1 reports the entrance data. About one in four applicants

**Table 1. University of Washington Early Entrance Program 1977–1981\***

236 students took the Washington PreCollege Test.
59 qualified for EEP.
44 registered for one or more courses.

1 has graduated
20 are undergraduates in good standing at UW.
11 withdrew after sampling only one UW course.
7 withdrew after sampling two or more UW courses.
3 have transferred in good standing to other colleges or universities.
2 remain in high school and are supplementing their high school program.

*Radical accelerants only (qualified by age 14) by Fall Quarter, 1981.

qualified on the Washington PreCollege Test (WPCT), but the mutual selection process further narrows the group so that about one in ten actually enters the program.

Having qualified initially, students may enter the EEP program via either of two paths. Until 1980, the single route for entry was engagement in increasingly demanding university course loads while simultaneously maintaining a major involvement in another home school, usually a junior high school. Students were encouraged to begin with courses in their favored area of interest and preparation, but by the time a full probationary quarter was undertaken, the selection of courses had to represent a broad spectrum. Such courses would eventually be needed to meet distribution and other college requirements. A grade point average of 3.0 or better during the probationary quarter was required to qualify for full admission to the EEP. Ordinarily that quarter was taken in the summer, so that, if a student did not seem to be profiting from the program, no bridges had been burned and the standard secondary school educational track had not been interrupted. This system had the advantage of providing the student with a gradual entry into the university, but most students found it difficult to cope with the kind of "split personality" required in trying to adapt to two school settings and to manage scheduling and transportation problems. Moreover, the massive grade skipping represented by this program left some obvious gaps in the students' survival skills for coursework at the university level.

For these reasons, a transition component, or bridge, was added to the Early Entrance Program in 1980–1981. Consisting in essence of a minischool, the small program for thirteen to fifteen students concentrates explicitly on the skills needed by college freshmen. It also provides a convenient base (geographic and personal) from which the student may take regular university coursework as appropriate. Instruction centers on writing style, organizing material, preparing term papers, taking blue book exams, notetaking, typing, review procedures and other study skills, as well as basic concepts in science and the humanities. In addition, content areas such as mathematics (up to the precalculus course taught at the university), history, literature, and foreign language are included. A full time coordinator and several part time teachers and tutors (ranging from regular university faculty to graduate students and even Early Entrance Program students ("EEP'ers") provide a selective education. The goal of the transition component is an accelerated program that breeds confident, competent, organized, and mature students. Its first graduates have just joined the EEP so it is too early to be certain, but it is our impression that the program is a more effective support for the young student in transition into the university than was the alternative (and intact) method.

For students enrolled in courses at the university, the EEP provides a comprehensive support system. All first year students are required to attend a weekly meeting that provides a chance to make friends and to share problem solving and information. The meetings give program staff a chance to troubleshoot, as individual or common issues become apparent. The meetings also serve the instructional program of the university by introducing coleaders, clinical psychology interns, and child psychiatry fellows to a gifted population. In addition to the regular meetings, which many students attend far past the required four quarters, the program provides a lounge and study area to be used as home base between classes. Each student who is not yet affiliated with a major department is also required at least quarterly to discuss academic plans in preparation for registration, and all EEP undergraduates are asked to set aside another hour per quarter for discussion of more personal adjustment matters.

In addition to these required elements of the program, however, it is the availability of staff and their sensitivity to students' behavioral clues that permit effective support and intervention as needed. Students who begin to come around more often or less often, who actively seek help in dealing with academic problems or suddenly become vague in talking about their courses, who appear glum or suddenly become silly and attention seeking, as well as those students who drop by to chat about anticipated, emerging, and/or minor concerns about which they are developing increasingly mature coping skills — all these constitute an ongoing responsibility of the program staff. Most of these young people were at least mildly unhappy in their school situation before they entered the EEP. Indeed, this state of affairs was the most predominant reason behind their choice of this particular educational alternative, or compromise, rather than another.

The EEP acts in a more parental role than is common in universities today, but in addition it works closely with parents. Students live at home for their first two years at least, and most families are active partners with EEP in monitoring and supporting the work and play of their students. One of the most difficult problems confronting many families is the rapid social and personal maturation of their children in a telescoped time. The metamorphosis from child to college student occurs more rapidly than the parents had anticipated. Most, but not all, families have been able to make this transition with good grace. One retired father still accompanies his son, now a senior, to class and back every day; others drive to and fro students who are perfectly capable of taking the bus. Some find it difficult to refrain from calling professors to discuss their children's progress or to voice complaints. Some still argue about bedtimes and baths.

Despite the contrast in age between EEP students and their classmates, our overall impression of the social adjustment of these students is quite positive. Many have continued their extracurricular activities, such as the serious pursuit of a foreign language, ballet and swimming, orchestra and solo musical instruments. Some have joined campus activities such as the marching band, the crew, the sailing club, the campus newspaper, and various student political groups. Most seem to have satisfying friendships both within the program and outside it. It is our impression that the girls, who tend to be well into puberty when they enter the program, have an easier time socially than the boys, particularly the prepubescent boys. Fortunately, prepubescence is a temporary affliction, and we witness a marked leap in the social skills and maturity of these youngsters as the years go by.

With regard to the academic achievement of the students, the record is very presentable. Table 2 reports in capsule form the standing and academic progress of the group through Spring Quarter, 1981. (Average grade point average at this university approaches 3.0 where 4.0 is maximum).

One student, a fifteen-year-old classics major, graduated from the program in 1981. She has decided to remain at the university to pursue a master's in the same area, while she simultaneously obtains advanced training in ballet. Several others are due to graduate in 1982. Students are encouraged to pursue a well-rounded liberal arts education in addition to a specific course of study. Moreover, they must meet special University requirements because of having entered without the usual high school prerequisites. The typical student will probably take about five years to graduate. Several, tempted intellectually in many directions at once (usually despite our advice), carry course loads of

### Table 2. University of Washington Early Entrance Program Status of Radical Accelerants After Spring Quarter, 1981

| Level | N | Average Total U.W. Credits | Grade Point[a] |
|---|---|---|---|
| Freshman (0–44 Credits) | 2 | 42.0 | 3.62 |
| Sophomore (45–89 Credits) | 6 | 57.2 | 3.57 |
| Junior (90–134 Credits) | 5 | 109.8 | 3.49 |
| Senior (135+ Credits) | 6 | 160.0 | 3.58 |
| (Total Undergraduate) | (19) | (99.7) | (3.56) |
| Transfers (at time of departure) | 3 | 76.7 | 3.56 |
| Graduate | 1 | 180.0 | 3.41 |

[a]Maximum = 4.0. Average undergraduate grade = 3.0.

over 20 credits each quarter, rather than the usual 15 units, because there is so much they want to learn. These are by and large "turned on" students — eager, industrious, organized, and successful. Most of them are contemplating graduate work upon completion of their undergraduate degrees, with career aspirations distributed over a broad spectrum. We have students who are currently headed for international corporate law, space exploration, medicine, geophysics, drama, music composing, computer science, writing novels, business administration, mathematics, the diplomatic corps, engineering, and college teaching/research in a variety of areas.

To return to our earlier theme, it is important to stress that the philosophy underlying the Early Entrance Program is not acceleration per se but an optimal match between the student and the learning situation. EEP students have demonstrated, before entering the program, the maturity, a good many of the skills, and most of the knowledge needed for success in college. Many of them have had to scramble along the way to pick up missing skills and content, but for the most part they have been able to accomplish this easily. (One twelve-year-student with only one year of high school algebra, largely self-taught, followed literally the advice of her calculus teaching assistant to "take a weekend to read a trigonometry text," for example.) Their curiosity, verve, and optimism reflect for the most part the kind of match for which the program was designed, though monitoring that match must be done more carefully than would be the case for ordinary freshmen.

Some students have had academic problems along the way; some, in fact have withdrawn. (See Table 1.) By no means all those who have withdrawn have earned poor grades; rather they have tried the EEP as an experiment and have opted for another alternative. We have not yet in error admitted any students who were not bright enough to handle this program. We have, however, witnessed several students who have had trouble for other reasons. We have not developed a set of rules of thumb that characterize students who will succeed with ease in the EEP versus those who will find the adjustment more troublesome. These characteristics match very closely those described by Stanley (1981) in his description of successful younger students at Johns Hopkins University:

1. Demonstration of a very high general ability according to the Washington PreCollege or other test scores. General achievement at least equal to that of older university students is essential. In the course of meeting college requirements, students with distinctive patterns of ability sometimes encounter specific courses with which they have difficulty, but they do very well in their major fields. Those who have the easiest time, however, have demonstrated high levels of competence in both verbal and quantitative fields.

2. A consistent pattern of good grades in the previous school setting. The student who, though bored, has made an effort to comply with conventional school demands, is likely to accept with relatively good grace the occasional mediocre professor, the disliked assignment, or the unwelcome distribu-

tion requirement and to apply himself or herself with sufficient energy to maintain a good record.

3. High motivation to enter the EEP. The capable student who contacts us independently, who eagerly desires not just to escape from the current school but to partake of what the university offers, is usually able to do so successfully.

4. Relatively positive mental health, though not necessarily popularity or contentment, in the previous school. The student with adjustment problems at entry may well have difficulty dealing with the demands of this challenging program and may be hampered by poor problem-solving and interpersonal skills.

5. Habits of industry, organization, and application. Students who have filled their lives outside of school with so many activities that they have had to maintain strong self-discipline and consistent organization do well with us. Typical outside activities of such students have included playing more than one musical instrument, serious modern dance and ballet, swimming, skiing, studying several foreign languages, writing poetry, earning spending money with paper routes, and so on. The student who tells us that reading or another passive pursuit is the favorite hobby may be in for trouble.

6. Competitiveness, preferably oriented toward improving one's own record rather than beating the opposition. Students who have engaged in activities that require constant improvement (such as dance, competitive individual sports, playing instruments, and learning languages) often develop habits of perseverance in the face of adversity and discouragement. They would not acquire such habits in the ordinary school situation where the work is easy. We have witnessed several students whose previous unremitting successes had ill-prepared them to meet the challenge of the optimal educational match. Accustomed to doing beautifully with a minimum of personal investment, they have found highly aversive the need to work hard and have been overly alarmed by occasional medium to low grades on examinations or papers. Cutting class, postponing assignments, and failing to review for examinations, they have fallen behind and compounded the assault on their feelings of self-worth and competence.

7. Families who encourage academic excellence and support the student's entry into EEP. When one parent or the other is subtly opposed to the program, trouble brews. The dissenting parent often makes demands that are incompatible with steady application on the part of the student. Fortunately, even though this situation sometimes exists initially, it usually diminishes once the EEP'er begins to thrive. Our families range from those of very modest means and modest education to highly educated professional couples. Although a well-educated family usually provides an intellectual context that is conducive to academic success, it is the combined purposiveness, respect, and support offered by the parents that appear to be crucial.

8. Parental harmony and mental health. Marital discord, divorce, and

parental mental illness produce as much havoc with our students as they would with any other teenagers. In every case in which a student has exhibited marked difficulty in our program, there has been serious trouble at home unrelated to the EEP. When students' resources must be diverted to a more personal agenda, particularly when that agenda involves the parents, there may not be enough energy left to cope with the academic challenge.

Any program of this nature must be flexible and experimental. Currently, for example, the transition component curriculum is undergoing refinement and fine tuning with feedback as its graduates encounter the demands of university courses. The admissions procedure for both the Early Entrance Program and the transition component are being formalized, to include the usual transcripts (very high grades required) and letters of reference, additional data (the Wechsler Adult Intelligence Scale, Revised) and focused extensive interviews.

A grant from the William H. Donner Foundation of New York will make possible a comprehensive and objective assessment of the personal and social adjustment of the EEP students. It is clear that, as a group, they have been successful students at the University of Washington and at the demanding colleges (Duke University, Reed College, California Institute of Technology) to which a few have transferred. How well, though, are they managing their lives? Thus far, we have only subjective impressions.

During the next three years, EEP students who have entered the program since late 1979 will be compared with three groups of students: (1) those who qualified for the program but did not elect to join in, (2) regular University of Washington students matched for Washington PreCollege Test scores (taken, on the average, when four to five years older), and (3) regular University of Washington students who present exceptionally high Washington PreCollege Test scores. In other words, the EEP students will be compared with nonaccelerated high school students and college students who are equally bright and with another group of college students who are not as exceptional in intelligence but who are equally ready for the college coursework as judged by their WPCT scores.

Most of the evidence collected will be questionnaire measures, annually administered over a three-year period and covering the following areas:

1. Intellectual ability (Washington PreCollege Test Scores, Terman Concept Mastery Test).
2. Overall personal adjustment (MMPI, IPAT Anxiety Questionnaire).
3. Personality descriptions (California Test of Personality, Tennessee Self-Concept Scale, Locus of Control questionnaire, Personal Orientation Inventory).
4. Social relations (Dating Problems Checklist, Social Performance Survey Schedule, structured interview).
5. Maturity (Bem Sex-Role Inventory, Defining Issues Test, assessment of career decision making).
6. Academic Performance (transcripts, Graduate Record Examination).

Information about the students' in-class behavior will be sought from instructors, and parents will be asked to describe the adjustment of their children as well. The thrust of the study is descriptive, although the comparison of the responses of the radically accelerated students with the various nonaccelerated groups will be instructive. Confounded variables are unavoidable. The radical accelerants, for example, are probably a less satisfied group of students when they apply to the program than are those who apply but elect not to join it, although they may also be more confident of their ability to succeed in a challenging situation. The groups may differ in family background and family goals, in education experience, and in social skills. The broad range of information to be gathered over a three-year period will yield, it is hoped, not only descriptive material but a set of hypotheses for further exploration.

It is, of course, too early to evaluate the outcome of a program of this nature. The ultimate personal and professional careers of these highly talented young people will constitute the best index of the appropriateness of their having participated in a program of radical acceleration. It is unfortunate indeed that Hal Robinson will not be here to follow, as he enthusiastically anticipated, these gifted and promising young people as they enter adulthood. So far, however, the evidence indicates that the program he conceived will continue as a memorial to a psychologist who cared very deeply about what he could do for these young people and what they could, in turn, do for their society.

## References

Austin, A. B., and Draper, D. C. "Peer Relationships of the Academically Gifted: A Review." *Gifted Child Quarterly,* 1981, *25,* 129–133.

Congdon, P. J. "Helping Parents of Gifted Children." In J. J. Gallagher (Ed.), *Gifted Children: Reaching Their Potential.* Jerusalem: Kollek and Son, 1979.

Daurio, S. P. "Educational Enrichment Versus Acceleration: A Review of the Literature." In W. C. George, S. J. Cohn, and J. C. Stanley (Eds.), *Educating the Gifted: Acceleration and Enrichment.* Baltimore, Md.: Johns Hopkins University Press, 1979.

Freeman, J. *Gifted Children.* Baltimore, Md.: University Park Press, 1979.

Gallagher, J. J. *Teaching the Gifted Child.* (2nd ed.) Boston: Allyn & Bacon, 1979.

Gold, M. J. *Education of the Intellectually Gifted.* Columbus, Ohio: Merrill, 1965.

Greenspan, S. "Social Intelligence in the Retarded." In N. Ellis (Ed.), *Handbook of Mental Deficiency: Psychological Theory and Research.* (2nd ed.) Hillsdale, N.J.: Erlbaum, 1979.

Hildreth, G. H. *Introduction to the Gifted.* New York: McGraw-Hill, 1966.

Hobson, J. R. "High School Performance of Underage Pupils Initially Admitted to Kindergarten on the Basis of Physical and Psychological Examinations." *Educational and Psychological Measurement,* 1963, *23,* 149–170.

Hollingworth, L. S. *Children Above 180 IQ.* New York: World Book, 1942.

Hunt, J. McV. *Intelligence and Experience.* New York: Ronald Press, 1961.

Hurst, J. G. "The Meaning and Use of Difference Scores Obtained Between the Performance on the Stanford-Binet Intelligence Scale and the Vineland Social Maturity Scale." *Journal of Clinical Psychology,* 1962, *18,* 153–160.

Keating, D. P. (Ed.) *Intellectual Talent: Research and Development.* Baltimore: Johns Hopkins University Press, 1976.

Keating, D. P. "The Acceleration/Enrichment Debate: Basic Issues." In W. C. George, S. J. Cohn, and J. C. Stanley (Eds.), *Educating the Gifted: Acceleration and Enrichment.* Baltimore: Johns Hopkins University Press, 1979.

Kett, J. "History of Age Grouping in America." In J. S. Coleman and others (Eds.), *Youth: Transition to Adulthood. A Report to the Panel on Youth of the President's Science Advisory Committee.* Chicago: University of Chicago Press, 1974.

Meyers, C. E., Nihira, K., and Zetlin, A. "The Measurement of Adaptive Behavior." In N. Ellis (Ed.), *Handbook of Mental Deficiency: Psychological Theory and Research.* (2nd ed.) Hillsdale, N.J.: Erlbaum, 1979.

Newland, T. E. *The Gifted in Socioeducational Perspective.* Englewood Cliffs, N.J.: Prentice-Hall, 1976.

Painter, E. "A Comparison of Achievement and Ability in Children of High Intellectual Potential." Unpublished master's thesis, London University, 1976.

Robinson, H. B. "The Case for Radical Acceleration." In C. P. Benbow and J. C. Stanley (Eds.), *Academic Precocity: Aspects of Its Development, Consequences, and Nurturance.* Baltimore, Md.: John Hopkins University Press, forthcoming.

Rothman, E., and Levine, M. "From Little League to Ivy League." *Educational Forum,* 1963, *28,* 29–34.

Stanley, J. C. "Using the SAT to Find and Help Youths Who Reason Extremely Well Mathematically: A Report on the Johns Hopkins University Program." Address presented at the annual meeting of the American Educational Research Association, Los Angeles, April 13, 1981.

Stanley, J. C., Keating, D. P., and Fox, L. H. (Eds.). *Mathematical Talent: Discovery, Description, and Development.* Baltimore, Md.: Johns Hopkins University Press, 1974.

Terman, L. M. *Genetic Studies of Genius: Mental and Physical Traits of a Thousand Gifted Children.* Vol. 1. Stanford, Calif.: Stanford University Press, 1925.

Terman, L. M. and Oden, M. G. *Genetic Studies of Genius. The Gifted Child Grows Up: Twenty-five Years' Follow-Up of a Superior Group.* Vol. 4. Stanford, Calif.: Stanford University Press, 1947.

*Nancy M. Robinson is current director of the CDRG and completed this chapter based on available materials.*

*Halbert B. Robinson, former director of the University of Washington Child Development Research Group (CDRG), died March 25, 1981.*

# Index

## A

Allport, D. A., 51, 57
Armstrong, M., 8, 13, 27
Arnheim, R., 27
"At promise," concept of, 49–50, 55
Austin, A. B., 85, 93

## B

Baldwin, A. L., 3, 4
Bamberger, J., 61–77
Bandura, A., 43
Barron, F., 17, 27
Belo, J., 48, 58
Bever, T., 52, 58
Block, J. N., 49, 58
Brand, M., 9–10, 27
Braverman, H., 22, 27
Bringuier, J., 43
Brody, N., 37, 44
Bronfenbrenner, U., 3, 4
Brooks, L. D., 49, 58

## C

Cantor, G., 41–42
Carey, S., 61*n*
Carnegie Corporation, 47*n*
Case, R., 43
Changeux, J. P., 54, 58
Chase, W., 18, 27
Chen, E., 49, 58
Chicago, University of, early entry to, 86
Child Development Research Group, 79*n*, 86
Chomsky, N., 53, 58
Clausen, J. A., 2, 4
Coincidence, and giftedness and creativity, 36–37
Cole, M., 53, 58
Commons, M., 16, 27
Competence: domains as spheres of, 51–53; intellectual, 52
Congdon, P. J., 82, 93
Conservation, and development, 17

Cottrell, L., 3
Cowan, P., 31, 43
Creativity: Case studies scarce on, 18; cognition and affect in, 23–26; genius, giftedness, and, 41; giftedness related to, 7–29; and interactions, 33, 34–37; kinds of, 40–41; knowledge of, embryonic, 17–18; and known creators, 15–16; loosely coupled systems in, 21–23; and psychometric approach, 17; research strategies for linking giftedness and, 15–16; and stages, 33, 34, 37–39; and transition, 33, 39–42; work and play in, 22
Csikzentmihalyi, M., 12, 17, 27

## D

Damon, W., 43
Danchin, A., 54, 58
Darwin, C., 18, 21, 23–24, 40
Daurio, S. P., 82, 84, 93
Denenberg, V., 54, 58
Dennis, M., 54, 58
Development: concept of, 6; of domains, 53–55; environment and heredity interacting in, 13–15; evolving systems approach to, 20–26; framework for research on, 31–45; knowledge of, incomplete, 16–17; and life cycle stages, 16; pathways of, 11–12; problems in study of, 16–20; research on process of, 15; unilinear theories of, 16; and universals, 16–17
DeVries, R., 36, 44
Dines, A. M., 27
Divergent thinking, and creativity, 12, 17
Dobzhansky, T., 14, 27
Domains: development of, 53–55; separate, concept of, 50–51; as spheres of competence, 51–53
Donner Foundation, William H., 92
Draper, D. C., 85, 93
Dukas, H., 26, 28
Dworkin, G., 49, 58